The History of Egypt

CRAFTED BY SKRIUWER

Copyright © 2025 by Skriuwer.

All rights reserved. No part of this book may be used or reproduced in any form whatsoever without written permission except in the case of brief quotations in critical articles or reviews.

At **Skriuwer**, we're more than just a team—we're a global community of people who love books. In Frisian, "Skriuwer" means "writer," and that's at the heart of what we do: creating and sharing books with readers worldwide. Wherever you are in the world, **Skriuwer** is here to inspire learning.

Frisian is one of the oldest languages in Europe, closely related to English and Dutch, and is spoken by about **500,000 people** in the province of **Friesland** (Fryslân), located in the northern Netherlands. It's the second official language of the Netherlands, but like many minority languages, Frisian faces the challenge of survival in a modern, globalized world.

We're using the money we earn to promote the Frisian language.

For more information, contact : **kontakt@skriuwer.com** (www.skriuwer.com)

TABLE OF CONTENTS

CHAPTER 1: INTRODUCTION

- Geographic overview and the role of the Nile
- Key historical themes shaping Egypt's identity
- Chronological framework and major eras

CHAPTER 2: PREHISTORIC EGYPT

- Transition from hunter-gatherers to settled farming
- Earliest human activity along the Nile Valley
- Foundations for later cultural development

CHAPTER 3: THE PREDYNASTIC PERIOD

- Distinct regional cultures (Badari, Naqada, Maadi-Buto)
- Increasing social complexity and craft specialization
- Momentum toward political unification

CHAPTER 4: THE EARLY DYNASTIC PERIOD

- First pharaohs establishing centralized rule
- Emergence of royal iconography and administration
- Consolidation of Upper and Lower Egypt

CHAPTER 5: THE OLD KINGDOM

- Construction of pyramids as state-sponsored projects
- Heightened pharaonic power and religious ideology
- Economic and social structures supporting large-scale building

CHAPTER 6: THE FIRST INTERMEDIATE PERIOD

- Collapse of Old Kingdom's central authority
- Local rulers and nomarchs vying for power
- Social and cultural shifts amidst political fragmentation

CHAPTER 7: THE MIDDLE KINGDOM

- Reunification under strong pharaohs
- Administrative reforms and bureaucratic efficiency
- Literary and artistic achievements reflecting a stable society

CHAPTER 8: THE SECOND INTERMEDIATE PERIOD

- Another breakdown of centralized power
- Hyksos dominance in the Delta and Theban resistance
- Struggle leading to eventual reunification under Thebes

CHAPTER 9: THE NEW KINGDOM

- Egypt's imperial expansions and military campaigns
- Famous rulers like Hatshepsut, Thutmose III, and Ramses II
- Vast temple-building and flourishing trade networks

CHAPTER 10: THE THIRD INTERMEDIATE PERIOD

- Decline after the New Kingdom's peak
- Rise of Libyan and Nubian influences in rulership
- Fragmented political landscape and shifting alliances

CHAPTER 11: THE LATE PERIOD

- Saite Dynasty's attempts at cultural revival
- Growing threats from regional powers, especially Persia
- Reform efforts in administration and military organization

CHAPTER 12: THE PERSIAN CONQUEST AND AFTERMATH

- *Persian rule and local revolts against foreign domination*
- *Periods of Persian withdrawal and return*
- *Ultimate replacement by Alexander the Great's forces*

CHAPTER 13: THE GRECO-ROMAN PERIOD

- *Ptolemaic dynasty blending Greek and Egyptian traditions*
- *Alexandria as a hub of learning and commerce*
- *Transition to Roman governance and gradual Christian influence*

CHAPTER 14: CHRISTIAN EGYPT AND THE COPTIC ERA

- *Emergence and spread of Christianity under Roman rule*
- *Formation of the Coptic Church with its Miaphysite stance*
- *Monastic movements and religious debates shaping society*

CHAPTER 15: THE ARAB CONQUEST OF EGYPT

- *End of Byzantine control through Islamic expansion*
- *Introduction of new administrative and religious frameworks*
- *Foundations for centuries of Islamic governance*

CHAPTER 16: THE FATIMID ERA

- *Isma'ili Shi'a caliphate centered in Cairo*
- *Cultural and architectural achievements under Fatimid patronage*
- *Decline paving the way for other Islamic dynasties*

CHAPTER 17: THE AYYUBID AND MAMLUK PERIODS

- Saladin's Sunni restoration and anti-Crusader campaigns
- Rise of the Mamluk military elite and their sultanate
- Monumental building, scholarship, and defense against Mongols

CHAPTER 18: THE OTTOMAN PERIOD

- Egypt as an Ottoman province governed by appointed pashas
- Residual Mamluk power and local autonomy within imperial structures
- Gradual weakening of centralized Ottoman authority

CHAPTER 19: EGYPT UNDER MUHAMMAD ALI AND HIS SUCCESSORS

- Sweeping military and economic reforms forging modern institutions
- Heightened foreign involvement and projects like the Suez Canal
- Attempts at modernization under a hereditary dynasty

CHAPTER 20: CONCLUSION

- Major themes of resilience, cultural synthesis, and the Nile's continuity
- Review of Egypt's transitions from ancient times through the 19th century
- Reflections on the enduring legacy of Egyptian history

CHAPTER 1

INTRODUCTION

Egypt is a land of vast deserts, a life-giving river, and a history that stretches back thousands of years. When many people think about Egypt, they picture towering pyramids, mummified pharaohs, and the Great Sphinx. They might also recall famous historical figures like Tutankhamun, Ramses II, or Cleopatra. Yet the history of Egypt goes much deeper than just these well-known images. There are many periods that helped shape ancient Egypt into a complex and enduring civilization. This chapter sets the stage for our detailed journey into the past.

1.1. Geographic Setting

The geography of Egypt is shaped above all by the Nile River. This river runs from south to north, cutting through deserts on either side. Ancient Egyptians sometimes called their land Kemet, meaning the "black land," because the Nile would flood annually, depositing dark, fertile silt on the fields. Meanwhile, they called the desert Deshret, meaning the "red land." The contrast between fertile soil and harsh desert helped shape the mindset and the activities of the people. Life was concentrated along the river. Most people depended on farming, fishing, and limited trade.

Because desert lands surrounded the Nile on both sides, this natural barrier offered some protection from outside invasions in early times. Still, over the centuries, various groups did manage to enter and sometimes control Egypt. But in general, the deserts made long-term settlement for foreigners difficult unless they adapted to the Nile-centric lifestyle.

1.2. The Concept of Dynastic Egypt

Throughout the book, we will refer to dynasties. A dynasty is a sequence of rulers from the same family or lineage. Ancient Egyptian historians, notably Manetho, who was an Egyptian priest in the Ptolemaic period, divided the rulers of Egypt into 30 or 31 dynasties. This system allows us to group sets of kings and show how political power changed hands over time. The earliest dynasties emerged around the end of what we now call the Predynastic Period, and some dynasties extended well into later times.

The history of these dynasties is not always straightforward. Kings sometimes ruled at the same time in different parts of the country. Some dynasties overlapped, and historians still argue about the order of some kings. Even so, the idea of dynasties helps us follow how Egypt's leadership changed through the centuries.

1.3. Sources of Egyptian History

Our knowledge of ancient Egypt comes from several sources. First, there are archaeological discoveries such as tombs, temples, and items buried with the dead. These items often contain hieroglyphic inscriptions. Hieroglyphs were the picture-based writing system used by ancient Egyptians. Stones, walls, and papyrus scrolls feature texts that discuss religion, business transactions, literature, and more. Each discovery adds to our understanding of how the people lived, believed, and governed.

Second, we learn from writings by ancient historians. Herodotus, a Greek historian from the 5th century BCE, wrote about his visit to Egypt. Though some of his accounts are filled with tall tales, they also offer glimpses into Egyptian customs. Other Greek and Roman writers, along with Jewish and early Christian sources, also wrote about Egypt.

Third, there are modern archaeological and scholarly studies that use advanced techniques such as carbon dating, DNA analysis, and digital reconstruction. These methods give us new insights into the chronology, the origins of certain populations, and the way society was organized.

1.4. Periodization of Egyptian History

We often split Egyptian history into broad periods:

- **Prehistory**: Before written records.
- **Predynastic Period**: When the foundations for ancient Egyptian civilization were laid.

- **Early Dynastic Period**: When the first rulers of a unified Egypt emerged.
- **Old Kingdom**: The age of the great pyramids.
- **First Intermediate Period**: A time of disunity and regional rule.
- **Middle Kingdom**: A period of reunification and cultural flowering.
- **Second Intermediate Period**: Another breakdown in centralized power, with foreign rulers like the Hyksos.
- **New Kingdom**: The empire-building phase when Egypt reached its greatest power.
- **Third Intermediate Period**: Decline of central authority and rise of foreign influences.
- **Late Period**: Resurgence of Egyptian power, followed by conquests by Assyrians and Persians.
- **Greco-Roman Period**: The arrival of Alexander the Great, the Ptolemies, and finally Roman rule.
- **Coptic and Early Christian Era**: Spread of Christianity and the development of the Coptic Church.
- **Arab Conquest and Islamic Egypt**: Starting in the 7th century CE, leading to new changes in religion and politics.
- **Fatimid, Ayyubid, Mamluk, and Ottoman Periods**: Shifts in power under various Islamic dynasties and powers.
- **Muhammad Ali's Rule**: Early 19th century reforms and modernization attempts.

In this book, we will touch on each of these periods in detail, explaining the major transitions, accomplishments, and hardships that defined them.

1.5. Themes in Egyptian History

1.5.1. Religion and Belief Systems

Religion was central to Egyptian life. The people believed in a pantheon of gods, each representing an aspect of life or nature. Ra was the sun god, Horus was associated with kingship, Osiris with the afterlife, and so on. Pharaohs were viewed as divine or semi-divine, bridging the gap between gods and humans. The afterlife was crucial in Egyptian religious belief, leading to elaborate funerary practices, including mummification and tomb-building.

1.5.2. Kingship and Government

The pharaoh was not just a ruler but was seen as the living embodiment of the god Horus on Earth. To disobey the pharaoh was to disobey the gods. Hence, government was heavily centralized whenever the pharaoh's power was strong. At other times, local officials, known as nomarchs, could become powerful in their regions, especially during the Intermediate Periods. The balance between centralized and local power shifted over time, influencing how the country was run.

1.5.3. Art, Architecture, and Culture

Egyptian art and architecture are some of the most recognizable in the world. Pyramids, temples, statues of gods, and obelisks stand out as lasting symbols of Egyptian culture. Their art followed specific conventions over millennia, focusing on order, clarity, and the representation of spiritual themes. Scenes of daily life, such as farming, fishing, and family gatherings, also appeared in tomb paintings.

1.5.4. Wars, Trade, and Foreign Influences

Egypt's history is shaped by both internal developments and outside contacts. Warfare with neighbors—like Nubia to the south, or the Libyans to the west—shaped borders and political alliances. Trade with regions across the Red Sea and Mediterranean introduced new materials, ideas, and goods. Foreign powers, including the Hyksos, Persians, Greeks, and Romans, each left a mark on Egypt's culture, economy, and people.

1.5.5. Societal Structure

Society in ancient Egypt was hierarchical. The pharaoh stood at the top. Below him were nobles, priests, and high officials. Scribes were also important because they could read and write, handling bureaucratic tasks. Craftsmen, traders, and farmers followed, with slaves or forced laborers at the bottom. Movement between classes was possible but not common. Family life centered on the home, with evidence suggesting that women had some legal rights, such as owning property.

1.6. Goals of This Book

In writing this book, the goal is to give a careful and detailed look at each major period in Egyptian history. We will examine how and why Egypt unified in the early periods, why it sometimes fragmented, and how it dealt with foreign invasions. We will also explore religious beliefs and how they changed, especially with the arrival of new powers and faiths. Finally, we will see how Egypt maintained its distinct culture despite the many transitions and conquests it experienced.

This study focuses on ancient and medieval history. While modern events are important, they are beyond the scope we aim to cover. Instead, we concentrate on the growth and evolution of the civilization from its earliest days up to the rule of Muhammad Ali in the early 19th century, stopping before the deep changes of the modern era. By doing so, we can give our full attention to the times when Egypt's unique identity was formed and refined.

1.7. Egypt's Lasting Impact

Even after thousands of years, the monuments and legacies of ancient Egypt continue to fascinate the world. Their system of writing, their study of geometry and astronomy for building the pyramids, and their complex religious texts have intrigued scholars for centuries. Egypt influenced Greece, Rome, and other ancient civilizations. Many later societies borrowed from or admired Egyptian architecture and iconography. Even if we only focus on older history, we can see how the seeds of many modern concepts—like the importance of record-keeping, religious unity, and state authority—took early root in this land by the Nile.

1.8. Scope and Structure

This book is divided into 20 chapters. Each chapter explores a specific period or theme, starting with Prehistoric Egypt and concluding with a chapter that sums up key points of Egypt's historical journey. Every chapter tries to paint a full picture without repeating earlier content. We will see the rise of leaders, the building of monuments, and the daily life of ordinary Egyptians. We will also note how foreign rulers adapted to local customs, or changed them, and the ways Egypt evolved yet kept its unique culture.

CHAPTER 2

PREHISTORIC EGYPT

Before the grand temples, mighty pharaohs, and towering pyramids, there were small groups of people who made their living by hunting, gathering, and eventually farming along the Nile. They did not build large monuments, and they left behind few written records—because writing had not yet been invented. Still, archaeology helps us piece together a picture of these earliest inhabitants and how they lived. This chapter covers what we know about these prehistoric communities, the environmental changes they faced, and how their gradual shift to farming prepared the ground for the rise of one of history's most famous civilizations.

2.1. The Nile's Early Environment

Today, we often picture the Sahara Desert as a dry, nearly lifeless expanse. But many thousands of years ago, large parts of what is now desert were grasslands with abundant wildlife. Climatic changes over millennia caused these areas to become more arid. As the climate dried, people and animals moved closer to water sources, particularly the Nile River. Over time, the river valley became a natural corridor for life, providing fish, plants, and drinking water.

Early groups likely moved seasonally, following animal migrations or searching for ripening plants. They made simple stone tools. Archaeological evidence in areas such as the Faiyum region and near the Nile's banks shows that people used flint to fashion blades, scrapers, and points. These tools were vital for hunting, preparing food, and making clothing.

2.2. Paleolithic Period (Before 10,000 BCE)

The Paleolithic, or Old Stone Age, is divided into the Lower, Middle, and Upper Paleolithic. During the Lower Paleolithic (around 2.5 million–300,000 years ago), early hominids such as Homo erectus roamed parts of Africa, including regions that would later become Egypt. Their stone tools were basic, like hand axes. Human populations were small and scattered.

In the Middle Paleolithic (about 300,000–50,000 years ago), Neanderthals and early Homo sapiens used more specialized stone tools. Sites in the Nile Valley suggest that these groups used the river's resources for survival. Over time, Homo sapiens became the dominant human type.

The Upper Paleolithic (about 50,000–10,000 years ago) brought more advanced tools and the first hints of cultural expressions, such as personal ornaments or primitive carvings. The climate was cooler, and parts of Africa were less arid than they are today. People lived in caves or open sites near the Nile or oases, using stone flakes to create tools for hunting gazelles, wild cattle, and other animals that lived in the grasslands.

2.3. The Late Paleolithic and Epipaleolithic (c. 20,000–10,000 BCE)

By the Late Paleolithic, people in the region had developed new ways of making tools. They used microliths, which were tiny stone blades used in composite tools like arrowheads or harpoons. These were attached to wooden or bone handles with resin or sinew. Fishing and gathering gained importance, as the Nile was home to many fish species, and the banks had edible plants.

Cultural developments continued, though we do not see large permanent settlements yet. People traveled in groups, taking advantage of seasonal resources. Cave art is rare in Egypt, but a few small rock art sites near the desert wadis (dry riverbeds) hint at prehistoric beliefs or rituals. We do not fully know what these drawings meant, but they feature animals and, in some cases, human figures or abstract designs.

2.4. Transition to the Neolithic (c. 10,000–5,000 BCE)

The Neolithic, or New Stone Age, started when humans began farming and domesticating animals. Around 10,000 BCE, the global climate warmed, leading to changes in rainfall patterns. In the region that includes today's Egypt, the Sahara began to dry even more. Populations moved closer to the Nile. Some of these groups started experimenting with planting wild grains or keeping herds of goats and sheep.

One key area for understanding early Egyptian farming is the Faiyum basin, west of the Nile. Here, archaeologists found evidence of cereals like wheat and barley, and remains of domesticated sheep and goats. Pottery shards also appear, which indicates storage and cooking methods had advanced. The presence of grinding stones suggests these communities ground grains into flour.

2.5. Early Settlements and Lifestyle

With farming, some groups could stay in one place longer. Small villages began to form, made up of simple huts or shelters built from reed, mud, or other materials. These early farmers still hunted and gathered, but domestic crops and animals gave them more stability. People stored surplus grains in baskets or pits, allowing them to plan for future needs.

Burial practices also changed in some areas. Cemeteries show that people were sometimes buried with personal items like jewelry made from shells or beads. This hints at the development of symbolic thought and possibly ideas about the afterlife or status in the community.

2.6. Tools and Pottery

As people settled more permanently, they refined their stone tool technology. Polished stone axes and sickle blades helped with farming. Pottery became a key part of daily life. Pots were used for cooking, storing water, and holding grains. Early pottery was hand-built and fired at low temperatures. Decorations were limited, often just simple lines or geometric patterns.

Over time, the quality of pottery improved. The spread of pottery techniques might have come from interactions with neighboring regions, such as the Levant. Trade or cultural exchanges could have introduced better methods of shaping, firing, and decorating pots. The presence of certain clay types or styles in distant regions suggests that people traveled and exchanged goods along the Nile or across desert routes.

2.7. Social Changes

Shifting from a nomadic lifestyle to a more settled one brought social changes. Populations grew, and people needed to develop ways to manage conflicts or organize communal tasks like irrigation. Though large-scale irrigation projects are more commonly associated with later periods, small-scale water management could have existed in Neolithic communities. Social hierarchies may have been rudimentary at first, but differences in wealth and status likely emerged with the accumulation of surplus food and specialized crafts.

The focus on fertility—of both the land and the people—might have influenced early religious ideas. Figurines or symbols that might represent fertility gods or goddesses show up in Neolithic sites across the Near East and Africa. We do not have clear evidence of structured temples or priests in this period, but rituals surrounding planting, harvesting, and burying the dead suggest that spiritual beliefs were starting to take shape.

2.8. Cultural Groups of the Neolithic in Egypt

Egypt's Neolithic was not a single, uniform culture. Different regions along the Nile had their own development. Some of the well-known groups include:

- **Faiyum A Culture**: This group occupied the Faiyum basin around the 5th millennium BCE. Archaeological finds include storage pits for grain, sickle blades, and simple pottery.
- **Merimde Culture**: Located in Lower Egypt (the northern region), Merimde sites show small-scale farming communities with round huts. They produced pottery and stone tools and buried their dead within settlements.
- **Badari Culture** (though this is often classified as Predynastic, it has roots in earlier Neolithic traditions): Located in Upper Egypt, it is known for high-quality pottery (including the distinctive black-topped ware), stone tools, and the earliest evidence of social stratification.

These groups are significant because they led directly into what we classify as the Predynastic Period. The ways they farmed, made tools, and buried their dead set patterns that would grow into full-blown Egyptian traditions.

2.9. The Domestication of Animals and Plants

By the late Neolithic, people in Egypt had domesticated sheep, goats, cattle, and possibly pigs. Cattle, in particular, became a sign of wealth and status, a practice that continued throughout ancient Egyptian history. Grains like emmer wheat and barley formed the core of the Egyptian diet, along with lentils, peas, and other crops. Over time, these staples would become central to Egypt's economy, feeding laborers who built pyramids and other monuments in later periods.

2.10. Rock Art and Early Beliefs

The deserts of western and southern Egypt contain prehistoric rock art depicting animals such as giraffes, elephants, and cattle. Many of these creatures no longer live in the region. This is evidence that the area used to be more hospitable. Some rock art shows scenes of people dancing or holding what appear to be ritual objects. Although interpretations vary, these images could suggest early religious ceremonies or communal gatherings.

As the land grew more arid, these groups might have migrated closer to the Nile or left the region altogether. But they took their culture and beliefs with them, eventually merging with or influencing the groups already settled along the river.

2.11. Connections with Neighboring Regions

Even in prehistoric times, the people of the Nile Valley did not live in isolation. They had contact with areas that are today the Sudan, Libya, and the Near East. Materials like obsidian or certain types of shells found in Egyptian sites came from distant places. This indicates the existence of trade or at least sporadic exchanges. It might have been through such interactions that the idea of domestication spread, or that pottery-making techniques improved.

2.12. Daily Life in Prehistoric Egypt

Although we have only fragments of evidence, we can piece together a rough idea of daily life:

- **Shelter**: Simple huts or shelters made from reeds, mud, or animal skins provided protection from heat and occasionally cold desert nights.
- **Clothing**: Likely made from animal hides. Later, as flax became cultivated, linen might have started to appear, although that is more documented in the Predynastic Period.
- **Food**: A mix of gathered wild plants, hunted game, fished resources from the Nile, and gradually more farmed produce like grains and legumes.
- **Tools**: Stone was shaped into sharp edges for cutting or scraping. Bones might have been used for needles or fishing hooks. Pottery vessels were made for cooking and storage.
- **Community Life**: People probably lived in small kin-based groups, cooperating in hunting or farming. Over time, leadership roles emerged to coordinate planting, harvesting, and storage.

2.13. Toward the Predynastic Period

By around 5,000–4,000 BCE, some of these Neolithic communities were moving into what we call the Predynastic Period. Differences in pottery styles, burial customs, and settlement organization become more pronounced. We see emerging regional cultures in Upper and Lower Egypt, each with its own identity. This gradual development set the stage for the eventual unification of Egypt under a single ruler.

The Badari culture in Upper Egypt is often viewed as a bridge between older Neolithic lifestyles and the more complex societies of the Predynastic era. Their burials sometimes contained grave goods like jewelry, decorated pottery, and figurines, suggesting that people were starting to differentiate social status in the afterlife.

2.14. Challenges of Prehistoric Study

One of the biggest challenges in studying Prehistoric Egypt is the lack of written records. We rely on material remains—tools, pottery, bones, and burial sites. Dating methods like radiocarbon dating help establish timelines, but there is still debate about the exact chronological boundaries. Also, shifting sands and the construction of modern cities and dams have destroyed or submerged many prehistoric sites. Archaeologists must piece together scattered findings to form a coherent narrative.

Despite these difficulties, the evidence shows that by the time we reach the late Neolithic, the people of the Nile Valley were on the path toward more complex social and political structures. The seeds of what would become ancient Egyptian religion, social hierarchy, and economic practices were already planted.

2.15. Environmental Shifts and Adaptation

Climate played a crucial role in shaping prehistoric Egyptian life. As rainfall patterns changed and the Sahara expanded, communities had to adapt or move. The Nile's flood cycle became essential for farming. Early Egyptians learned to observe these floods and plan their planting around them. This reliance on the river as a predictable water source gave them a stable base to develop farming and permanent settlements.

Over centuries, managing the floods and ensuring water distribution would become more organized, paving the way for state control in later dynastic times. But in the prehistoric phase, such structures were very localized. Villages or clusters of huts might have set up small irrigation channels or dikes, but large-scale projects were not yet possible or needed.

2.16. The Role of Domesticated Animals

Cattle, sheep, and goats provided food and possibly milk. Cattle were also significant in social and religious contexts. Rock art from the prehistoric Sahara frequently shows cattle, and some images hint at rituals involving these animals. The prominence of cattle continued into pharaonic times, with the cow goddess Hathor symbolizing motherhood and fertility. It seems that the deep respect for cattle had roots that reached back to prehistoric beliefs.

2.17. Early Trade Networks

While trade networks were not as extensive or formalized as they would become in dynastic times, prehistoric Egyptians did exchange goods and ideas. Stones that were not locally available, like obsidian or certain types of flint, traveled great distances. Shells from the Red Sea show up in sites far from the coast, suggesting either direct trade routes or chain-like exchanges among different communities. This exchange of objects likely also involved the exchange of culture—pottery styles, tool-making methods, and even proto-religious concepts.

2.18. Regional Variations

Prehistoric Egypt was not a monolith. The way of life in the delta region of Lower Egypt, with its marshes and abundant aquatic resources, differed from that in Upper Egypt's narrower valley. In the delta, fishing and waterfowl hunting might have been more prominent, while in Upper Egypt, reliance on farming and herding gradually increased. These variations set the stage for later cultural distinctions between the North (Lower Egypt) and the South (Upper Egypt), which played a part in the myths of unification and the symbolism of the crowns worn by pharaohs.

2.19. From Clans to Chiefdoms

Over thousands of years, prehistoric groups expanded from small family-based units to larger clan groups. Eventually, some groups may have formed chiefdoms, where a single leader had authority over multiple villages. This would be one step closer to the centralized state that emerged in the Early Dynastic Period. Evidence of larger, fortified settlements or specialized workshop areas suggests that some communities had more complex social structures and craft specialization.

2.20. The Legacy of Prehistoric Egypt

Though they left no grand monuments like the pyramids, prehistoric Egyptians set in motion the processes that made the dynastic civilization possible. They domesticated plants and animals, learned to manage the Nile's resources, developed basic crafts, and formed the social ties that later allowed for large-scale cooperation. Their spiritual beliefs, hinted at in burials and rock art, laid the groundwork for the complex religious worldview that would dominate dynastic Egypt for millennia.

2.20.1. Continuity into the Predynastic

In the coming chapters, especially the next chapter on the Predynastic Period, we will see how the roots planted in Prehistoric Egypt grew into distinct cultural identities. We will see the rise of the Badari and Naqada cultures, which began to produce more sophisticated pottery, elaborate grave goods, and eventually developed the social and political frameworks that led to the first kings.

2.20.2. Importance for Understanding All of Egyptian History

Studying prehistoric Egypt helps us understand why the civilization that arose along the Nile was unique. The challenges of the environment, the abundance provided by the river, and the interplay between different communities shaped the mindsets and practices of later Egyptians. Their reliance on the Nile's floods, their social organization around family and communal labor, and their religious outlook that tied life to the rhythms of nature all have their foundations in prehistory.

CHAPTER 3

THE PREDYNASTIC PERIOD

3.1. Overview of the Predynastic Period

The Predynastic Period in Egypt spans roughly from **5,000 BCE to around 3,100 BCE**, although the exact dates vary among scholars. During this era, different regional cultures developed along the Nile Valley before the country was unified under the first pharaohs. It was a time of innovation in agriculture, social structures, trade networks, religious ideas, and technological skills.

The growth of permanent settlements, craft specialization, and social stratification during this period set the groundwork for the Early Dynastic Period. While we covered the prehistoric roots in Chapter 2, here we see those roots evolve into more recognizable cultures—especially in the regions of **Upper Egypt** (the southern stretch of the Nile Valley) and **Lower Egypt** (the Nile Delta in the north).

3.2. Geographical and Cultural Divisions

One key aspect of the Predynastic Period is the noticeable cultural and geographical divide between **Upper Egypt** and **Lower Egypt**. Ancient Egyptians themselves recognized this division and later symbolized it through the "Two Lands," each with its own iconography and crown.

- **Upper Egypt (Southern Egypt)**: Narrow strips of arable land run alongside the Nile, surrounded by desert cliffs and rugged terrain. This geography often encouraged closely-knit communities.
- **Lower Egypt (Northern Egypt or the Delta)**: A broad region formed by the Nile branching into many channels. Its marshes and fertile fields supported fishing, farming, and transportation along waterways.

During the Predynastic Period, different cultures flourished in these two main zones. The interaction between them was often limited, but it grew over time. Eventually, as the process of unification began, leaders from Upper Egypt started to extend influence over the north.

3.3. Cultural Phases in Upper Egypt

3.3.1. Badari Culture (c. 4400–4000 BCE)

The **Badari Culture** is often considered a bridge between late Neolithic and true Predynastic societies. It centered around the **Asyut** region in **Upper Egypt**. Important sites include **el-Badari**, **Hammamia**, and **Matmar**. Archaeologists have found:

- **Black-topped pottery**: Characterized by red or brown surfaces with a distinct black rim. This pottery is well-made and suggests advanced firing techniques.
- **Stone tools and personal ornaments**: These show developing craftsmanship and some trade, as certain materials were not local.
- **Burials**: Graves often contained grave goods, such as jewelry, stone palettes, and pottery. The presence of grave goods indicates beliefs about an afterlife or at least concern for the deceased's well-being.

Social stratification during the Badari Period was not extreme, but differences in grave goods suggest that some individuals had higher status than others. Over time, the Badari Culture influenced later groups in Upper Egypt, including the Naqada cultures.

3.3.2. Naqada I (Amratian) Culture (c. 4000–3500 BCE)

After the Badari, the **Naqada I Culture** emerged, mostly in the region around **Naqada**, **Hierakonpolis**, and **Abydos**. This phase is also called the **Amratian Culture**. Its main traits include:

- **Refined pottery**: The black-topped style continued, but new types appeared, often decorated with wavy handles or incised patterns.
- **Stone palettes**: These started as functional items used to grind pigments (possibly for cosmetics or ritual). Over time, they became more decorative, sometimes shaped like animals or geometric designs.
- **Increasing craft specialization**: Evidence of dedicated workshops suggests that certain people specialized in pottery-making, stone-carving, or textile production.
- **Early trade networks**: Items like **obsidian** (from areas such as Ethiopia) and seashells (possibly from the Red Sea) point to growing exchange. Copper might also have begun to appear in small quantities, hinting at early metallurgy.

As with the Badari Culture, Naqada I burials often placed the deceased in pits with grave goods. However, the goods grew more varied and sometimes more elaborate. This indicates a slight expansion in social differences.

3.3.3. Naqada II (Gerzean) Culture (c. 3500–3200 BCE)

The **Naqada II**, or **Gerzean Culture**, shows a marked increase in complexity. Settlements became larger, and some sites appear to have gained regional importance. Notable trends include:

- **Painted pottery**: Pottery surfaces often feature **iconic motifs** such as boats, animals, and human figures. These painted scenes might reflect religious or symbolic themes.
- **Advanced stone palettes**: Decorative palettes reached new artistic heights, featuring animal-headed motifs and complex shapes. Some may have been used in rituals or displayed as status symbols.
- **Growing evidence of kingship or chieftainship**: Certain tombs at sites like **Hierakonpolis** or **Naqada** stand out for their size and the wealth of grave goods. This suggests powerful local leaders.
- **Expansion of trade**: More exotic goods—like **lapis lazuli** (likely from modern Afghanistan)—make appearances. The presence of such distant materials indicates long-range trade routes or intermediaries.
- **Emergence of symbols related to royalty**: Certain decorative elements, such as the **Horus falcon** or **Seth animal**, start to show up. Later, these become central to dynastic iconography.

Social stratification in Naqada II is more evident. Some graves are much richer than others, indicating that a ruling class or elite was forming. We also see hints of **warfare** or conflict in some depictions, such as scenes of boats with warriors, raising the possibility of territorial expansion or local power struggles.

3.3.4. Naqada III (Protodynastic) Culture (c. 3200–3000 BCE)

Sometimes referred to as the **Protodynastic Period**, **Naqada III** leads directly into the Early Dynastic Period. Key features are:

- **Emergent state structures**: The tombs at **Abydos** (Umm el-Qa'ab) show increasing complexity, with multiple chambers and prestige objects. These tombs may belong to the immediate predecessors of the First Dynasty kings.

- **Royal iconography**: Objects like the **Scorpion Macehead** or the **Narmer Palette** (though often dated right at the cusp between Naqada III and Early Dynastic) show the figure of a powerful ruler smiting enemies and wearing regalia that later becomes standard for pharaohs.
- **Growth of Hierakonpolis**: Excavations there reveal large-scale breweries, temple areas, and fortified structures, suggesting a significant urban center.
- **Proto-writing**: Some scholars argue that the earliest hieroglyphic signs appear on pottery or small labels in Naqada III contexts. These may have recorded ownership or the name of a ruler.

By the end of Naqada III, the consolidation of various local chiefdoms under a single ruler of Upper Egypt was nearly complete. These developments paved the way for the final push northward to unify Upper and Lower Egypt under one king in the Early Dynastic Period.

3.4. Cultural Phases in Lower Egypt

While Upper Egypt's Naqada cultures are well-documented, Lower Egypt had its own Predynastic developments, although evidence can be trickier to find due to the Delta's changing environment and water tables.

3.4.1. Maadi-Buto Culture

The **Maadi-Buto Culture** (named after sites like **Maadi** near modern Cairo and **Buto** in the Delta) thrived around **4000–3200 BCE**. Important aspects:

- **Mudbrick architecture**: Early use of mudbrick buildings suggests that Lower Egyptians had architectural innovations, possibly because wood was less available.
- **Copper usage**: Artifacts show that Maadi was a hub for copper trade. Copper ingots or tools from Sinai or the Levant might have traveled through Maadi.
- **Distinct pottery forms**: Compared to the black-topped or painted vessels in Upper Egypt, Maadi-Buto pottery tends to be simpler and utilitarian.
- **Trade connections**: The Delta region was closer to the Levant, making it a likely center for importing goods by sea or by overland routes across Sinai.

Lower Egypt also had local forms of social organization. However, by the time Naqada III rulers in Upper Egypt were growing stronger, some sites in Lower Egypt show signs of **Naqada influence** or direct control, hinting at the early stages of unification under southern elites.

3.5. Interaction and Trade Between Upper and Lower Egypt

During much of the Predynastic Period, Upper and Lower Egypt followed separate cultural paths. Yet, trade items such as **Basalt** or **Obsidian** found in Lower Egyptian sites, or Delta goods found in Upper Egyptian graves, show that contact existed. Over time, these contacts likely became more frequent and paved the way for political unification.

Trade was not only internal. **Exotic materials**—copper from Sinai, lapis lazuli from distant parts of Asia, gold from Nubia—flowed into the Nile Valley. Elite groups used these materials to assert status, while craft specialists transformed them into jewelry, ceremonial palettes, or ritual objects. Such wealth accumulation and control over trade routes bolstered the power of emerging leaders who could command labor and resources for prestige projects.

3.6. Religious and Symbolic Developments

In Chapter 2, we saw hints of early spiritual beliefs in prehistoric rock art and burials. By the Predynastic Period, religion was becoming more structured:

- **Animal cults**: Figures of animals like the falcon, cow, lion, and others appear frequently in art. Some of these became major deities in later periods (e.g., **Hathor** was sometimes represented as a cow, **Horus** as a falcon).
- **Funerary beliefs**: Burial customs grew more elaborate, especially for higher-status individuals. Graves often faced west (the direction of the setting sun), a tradition that carried on through dynastic times.
- **Symbolic palettes**: Large slate palettes may have been used in ritual contexts, with carved scenes depicting mythical or ceremonial events.
- **Sacred kingship**: The idea that a ruler could be divinely authorized took root. Art from Naqada III, such as the Scorpion Macehead, shows a figure wearing what might be the White Crown of Upper Egypt, emphasizing a near-divine status.

These religious and symbolic trends laid the groundwork for the complex Egyptian religion of the dynastic age, in which the **pharaoh** was seen as the intermediary between gods and humans.

3.7. Advances in Technology and Craftsmanship

3.7.1. Stoneworking

Predynastic artisans were adept at working **hard stones** like basalt, diorite, and granite. They fashioned bowls, vases, and ceremonial objects that required high levels of skill. Drilling holes in hard stone for vase handles or to create hollow interiors showed remarkable technical prowess.

3.7.2. Metalworking

Though not as widespread as in later eras, **copper** began to appear in tools, pins, and small ornamental items. Copper was hammered into shape or cast in molds. Over time, metal tools started to replace some stone implements, though stone tools remained common for a long time.

3.7.3. Pottery Innovations

Potters produced increasingly specialized forms. Painted pottery during Naqada II often depicted boats, birds, and geometric patterns. Some vessels from this period show advanced firing techniques for consistent coloration and durability.

3.7.4. Textiles and Basketry

Flax cultivation, important for making linen, likely expanded in the Predynastic Period. Linen would later be crucial for clothing and mummification wrappings. Baskets made from reeds or grass also were essential for storage and transport of grains, reflecting the agricultural lifestyle along the Nile.

3.8. Society and Social Structure

By the late Predynastic Period, society showed clear signs of **hierarchical organization**:

1. **Elites or Chieftains**: Individuals with access to luxury items, foreign goods, and elaborately furnished tombs.

2. **Craft Specialists**: Potters, stone carvers, metalworkers, and possibly scribes (toward the end of the period).
3. **Farmers, Herdsmen, and Laborers**: The bulk of the population engaged in agriculture, animal husbandry, and basic crafts.
4. **Slaves or Servants** (uncertain): The evidence for enslaved people is limited in Predynastic contexts, but forced labor or servitude may have existed, especially during major construction projects.

Power seemed to concentrate in the hands of those who controlled agricultural surplus, trade routes, and possibly local militias or armies. Burials often show the greatest wealth in Upper Egypt, suggesting that southern elites were more successful at gaining and displaying power.

3.9. The Rise of Urban Centers

While "cities" in the modern sense did not exist in Predynastic Egypt, certain sites grew larger and showed urban-like features:

- **Hierakonpolis (Nekhen)**: One of the most significant Predynastic centers in Upper Egypt. Archaeological findings reveal large-scale breweries, ceremonial structures, and a possible early temple area.
- **Naqada**: Gave its name to the Naqada cultures. The settlement and cemeteries show gradual growth in social complexity.
- **Abydos**: Home to important cemeteries. Future dynastic rulers of the Early Dynastic Period and beyond chose to be buried in or near Abydos, possibly for its long-standing religious significance.

These centers likely competed or formed alliances, paving the way for the dominance of a single polity. As one city gained an advantage over another—through trade, alliances, or military means—it expanded its influence. This process eventually led to broader political units that extended beyond local territories.

3.10. Early Expressions of Writing

Many scholars see the late Predynastic (Naqada III) as the time when the earliest forms of hieroglyphic writing begin to appear. Some small **labels** made of bone or ivory have **incised signs** that seem to represent names or places. This proto-writing might have been used for administrative purposes, like recording goods or identifying the owner of a container.

While true sentence-based hieroglyphic writing came slightly later, these simple markings are the direct ancestors of Egypt's famous script. The motivation behind developing writing was likely linked to **economic and political complexity**—tracking tribute, storing information about trade goods, and highlighting the power of emerging rulers.

3.11. Warfare and Military Organization

Depictions on some Predynastic pottery and palettes suggest **conflict**. Boats are shown with warriors, some carrying **maces** or **bows**. The so-called **Battlefield Palette** (though it might date to the very end of the Predynastic) shows prisoners, possibly captured in a military engagement. Fortifications or walls at places like Hierakonpolis may indicate that leaders recognized the need to defend resources or expand territory by force.

As local polities merged, leaders who could maintain a strong fighting force probably gained more influence. Control over the best farmland or trade routes might have triggered conflicts. Eventually, the strongest southern leaders emerged as the future kings of a unified Egypt.

3.12. The Final Steps to Unification

By the latter half of Naqada III, evidence points to a **single ruling authority** in Upper Egypt. Pottery styles and burial customs associated with Naqada III spread into parts of Lower Egypt, showing a cultural takeover. Rulers of Upper Egypt appear to have campaigned northward, conquering or absorbing local Delta polities.

Objects like the **Narmer Palette** (often considered the earliest historical document) show a king named **Narmer** wearing both the White Crown (Upper Egypt) and the Red Crown (Lower Egypt). While Narmer is usually seen as the figure who completed unification, he did not act in a vacuum. Generations of southern chieftains or proto-kings before him had paved the way.

3.13. Key Archaeological Discoveries

- **Tombs at Abydos**: These large tombs, some with multiple chambers, likely belong to predynastic kings or high elites. Over time, they grew in

complexity, signaling an evolution toward royal burials of the Early Dynastic and Old Kingdom.
- **Hierakonpolis Painted Tomb (Tomb 100)**: Contains the earliest known mural in Egypt, showing boats, figures, and possibly ritual scenes. This is a major clue about Predynastic religious and social life.
- **El-Gerzeh Cemetery**: A site that gave the name "Gerzean" to Naqada II culture, revealing advanced burial practices and a wealth of artifacts.
- **Maadi Settlement**: In Lower Egypt, offers insight into the lifestyles of northern communities with mudbrick houses, copper artifacts, and imported goods from the Levant.

These finds illustrate the shift from simple agrarian communities to larger, more hierarchical societies capable of impressive craftsmanship and centralized planning.

3.14. Daily Life in the Predynastic

Although most of our knowledge comes from tombs and settlements of the elite, some aspects of daily life can be reconstructed:

1. **Housing**: Common people likely lived in huts made of **wattle and daub**, reeds, or mudbrick. Permanent villages formed as agriculture became stable.
2. **Food and Agriculture**: Diet included bread made from **emmer wheat**, barley-based beer, vegetables, fruits (like dates and figs), and fish or meat when available.
3. **Clothing**: Men and women wore simple linen garments or wraparound skirts. Linen was lighter and well-suited for Egypt's hot climate.
4. **Family and Community**: Households centered around extended families. Tasks like planting, harvesting, or building new structures relied on communal labor.
5. **Religion and Ritual**: Simple shrines or household altars may have existed, but large temples were not yet a feature. Rituals involved offerings to deities or ancestors, seeking protection and a good harvest.

3.15. The Concept of Leadership

As populations grew, **leadership** became more formalized. Early on, local headmen or chieftains might have settled disputes and coordinated communal tasks. Over time, **status symbols** like special regalia, ceremonial maces, or distinctive clothing helped leaders show off their authority. Because the Nile environment required cooperation to manage floods and irrigation, strong leadership could unite communities and allocate labor. In times of conflict, a capable leader could also organize defenses or offensive campaigns.

By the late Predynastic, these leaders had grown into powerful kings with religious significance. They claimed the favor or descent from gods like **Horus**, marking the start of **divine kingship**, which would define pharaonic rule for over 3,000 years.

3.16. Transition to the Early Dynastic Period

The line between the end of the Predynastic Period and the **start of the Early Dynastic Period** (First and Second Dynasties) is somewhat blurred. **Narmer**, often cited as the first ruler of a united Egypt, stands at this junction. The unification process likely took decades, if not centuries, culminating around **3,100 BCE**.

During Naqada III:

- **Political centers**: Towns like **Hierakonpolis**, **Naqada**, and **Abydos** in Upper Egypt gained supremacy.
- **Military conquests**: Southern rulers subdued or assimilated Lower Egyptian communities.
- **Cultural assimilation**: Artistic styles, burial customs, and religious symbols of Upper Egypt spread northward, standardizing many cultural practices.

By the time Narmer's successors took the throne, the entire Nile Valley from the First Cataract (near modern Aswan) to the Mediterranean coast was nominally under one government. This centralized state, though still developing, laid the foundation for the dynastic periods to come.

3.17. Significance of the Predynastic Era

The Predynastic Period is crucial because it shows **how** and **why** Egypt was able to form such a long-lasting civilization. Key reasons include:

1. **Agricultural Abundance**: The Nile's predictable floods gave stable food supplies, which could support large populations.
2. **Trade Networks**: Control of trade routes, both within Egypt and abroad, concentrated wealth and power in the hands of a few.
3. **Social Stratification**: Over time, smaller communities became integrated under elite leaders, paving the way for the concept of kingship.
4. **Religious Unification**: Shared beliefs and symbols helped link communities culturally and spiritually, supporting the idea of a sacred monarchy.
5. **Technological Skills**: Mastery of stone, metal, pottery, and (in the last stages) proto-writing gave Predynastic Egyptians the means to organize large projects and complex economies.

3.18. Ongoing Debates and Research

Researchers still debate many aspects of this period. For example:

- **Exact Chronology**: Radiocarbon dates sometimes conflict with established sequences based on pottery styles.
- **Role of Conflict**: Was unification mostly peaceful through trade and alliances, or did warfare play a primary role?
- **Origins of Writing**: Some scholars believe that the earliest Egyptian writing might have been influenced by Mesopotamia, while others argue for an independent development.
- **Influence of Climate**: Shifts in rainfall and the expansion of desert areas likely spurred migration and cultural changes, but the details are still studied.

Continuing excavations in the Delta, along the Nile Valley, and in desert oases can provide new information about how local communities evolved and interacted. Each discovery, whether a single pot shard or an entire cemetery, can offer insights into the daily life, beliefs, and social structures of this formative age.

CHAPTER 4

THE EARLY DYNASTIC PERIOD

4.1. Introduction to the Early Dynastic Period

The **Early Dynastic Period** in Egypt, usually defined as **Dynasties 1 and 2**, spans approximately **3,100–2,686 BCE**. This era follows the Predynastic Period and marks the consolidation of power under the first historical pharaohs. It is the time when the rulers of a united Upper and Lower Egypt established many of the institutions, symbols, and traditions that defined pharaonic civilization.

Key themes include **the establishment of Memphis as a capital**, the evolution of **royal iconography** (crowns, scepters, regalia), and the standardization of religious concepts that positioned the king as a divine or semi-divine intermediary. During this period, the administration took shape, record-keeping advanced, and large-scale projects—especially royal tombs—set the stage for the monumental building that would come in the Old Kingdom.

4.2. King Narmer and the Unification of Egypt

While unification was a process that likely began in the late Predynastic era, tradition often credits **King Narmer** as the unifier. The famous **Narmer Palette**, discovered at **Hierakonpolis**, depicts him wearing both the **White Crown** of Upper Egypt and the **Red Crown** of Lower Egypt. Scenes on the palette show the king smiting enemies and controlling captives.

Whether Narmer was the first to unite the country or completed the work of earlier rulers like **Scorpion** (another proto-king) remains debated. However, Narmer's reign clearly symbolizes the dawn of a fully **integrated realm**. After his unification, rulers claimed to be "**Kings of Upper and Lower Egypt**," aligning themselves with the combined might and identity of the Two Lands.

4.3. The Founding of Memphis

One major achievement of these earliest pharaohs was the creation (or expansion) of a new administrative and political center—**Memphis**—near the boundary between Upper and Lower Egypt. Located at the apex of the Delta, Memphis sat at a strategic point for controlling trade, river traffic, and communication.

Tradition attributes Memphis's founding to the first king, sometimes referred to as **Menes** (a name that may refer to Narmer or his immediate successor, Hor-Aha). The city became a critical hub for:

- **Government administration**: Royal decrees, record-keeping, and the distribution of resources likely took place here.
- **Religious activities**: Temples dedicated to Ptah, one of the major creator gods, gained prominence in Memphis.
- **Craft production**: Artisans and scribes working for the court produced high-quality goods and official documents.

While **Abydos** in Upper Egypt remained an important religious center—especially for royal burials—Memphis grew into the heart of the political machine that ran the unified kingdom.

4.4. Royal Tombs of the Early Dynasties

4.4.1. Abydos Cemetery

The first two dynasties continued to build large and elaborate tombs at **Umm el-Qa'ab** in Abydos. Each king had a **mastaba** or a complex tomb structure. These tombs often included subsidiary burials of retainers who may have been sacrificed or buried to serve the king in the afterlife—though the exact practice of retainer sacrifice is still debated among Egyptologists.

Grave goods discovered in these tombs include:

- **Ivory labels** with early hieroglyphic inscriptions indicating regnal years or commodities.
- **Stone vessels** in large quantities.
- **Bead necklaces**, tools, and weapons, which showcased the wealth and power of the king.

The continuity of burying kings in Abydos underscores the **long-standing religious significance** of this region, which was associated with early gods and funerary beliefs.

4.4.2. Saqqara Necropolis

During the First and Second Dynasties, high officials and possibly some royals also built **mastaba tombs** at **Saqqara**, near Memphis. These mastabas had **rectangular** superstructures of mudbrick with **niched facades**, imitating palace architecture. Inside, multiple chambers stored goods for the afterlife.

Eventually, the **royal cemetery** would shift closer to Memphis during the Third Dynasty, culminating in the Step Pyramid of Djoser. But the tradition of burying high-ranking nobles at Saqqara already started in the Early Dynastic Period, showing the parallel development of major necropolises in both Upper and Lower Egypt.

4.5. Administration and Bureaucracy

As Egypt united, the pharaoh needed a system to govern distant provinces. We see the development of:

- **Scribes**: Trained in early hieroglyphics and **hieratic** (a cursive form of writing), scribes recorded taxes, inventories, harvests, and royal decrees.
- **Nomarchs**: The local governors of districts (called "nomes") who collected tribute and oversaw regional affairs.
- **Royal seal-bearers and treasurers**: Officials who managed the flow of goods—grain, cattle, precious materials—and distributed them to temples and work projects.

Titles such as **"Vizier"** may have already existed, indicating a top official directly under the king. Over time, these positions became more formalized, but the seeds of a structured bureaucracy were planted during Dynasties 1 and 2. The central authority used writing and seals to ensure accountability, with goods often marked by royal names or official titles.

4.6. Religion and Kingship in the Early Dynastic Period

One of the defining features of ancient Egypt was **divine kingship**—the idea that the king stood between the gods and humanity. In the Early Dynastic Period:

1. **Pharaoh's many names**: The practice of a king adopting multiple titles (Horus name, Nebty name, Golden Horus name, etc.) began to take shape. The **Horus name** associated the king with the falcon god, Horus.
2. **Royal iconography**: Crowns, including the White Crown (Upper Egypt) and Red Crown (Lower Egypt), or the combined **Pshent** (Double Crown), were used to show the king's dominion over the Two Lands.
3. **Temples and offerings**: While large temple complexes like Karnak were centuries away, smaller shrines existed, and the state began to standardize offerings to gods. The relationship between pharaoh, temple, and economy began to form.
4. **Mythology**: Stories of gods like **Osiris**, **Isis**, and **Horus** may have been forming in a more cohesive way, though the earliest textual sources appear later. Even so, the concept of the king as the living Horus and the deceased king as Osiris was already in motion.

4.7. Art and Architecture

Early Dynastic art continued many Predynastic traditions but became more standardized:

- **Sculpture**: Small-scale statues of kings or nobles appear, sometimes carved from hard stones. Although these are simpler than later statues, they lay the groundwork for the pharaonic style—frontal stance, idealized features, and formal poses.
- **Relief Carving**: Decorative palettes and maceheads used by royalty showcase scenes of victory, religious ceremonies, or processions. These reliefs, though still somewhat stylized, foreshadow the narrative reliefs of later periods.
- **Building Materials**: Mudbrick was still the primary material for most structures, but stone began to be used more often for certain temples or tomb elements. These experiments would lead to the grand stone monuments of the Old Kingdom.

4.8. Economy and Resource Management

The Early Dynastic kings oversaw a growing economy based on:

1. **Agriculture**: Emmer wheat, barley, flax, vegetables, and fruit were staple crops. Surplus grain was stored in state granaries, allowing the king to feed labor forces and officials.
2. **Livestock**: Cattle, sheep, goats, and pigs were common. The state might demand a **cattle count** as a form of tax or tribute, a practice that continued for centuries.
3. **Craft Production**: Workshops near the capital and in provincial centers produced pottery, textiles, and metal goods. Some items were for local use, while others showcased elite or royal status.
4. **Trade**: Contacts with Nubia to the south brought **gold**, **ebony**, and **exotic animal skins**. Trade with the Sinai region provided **turquoise** and **copper**. The Levant supplied cedar wood, resins, and possibly wine.

The royal court's control over these resources was a source of power. By redistributing goods to officials, temple staff, and local leaders, the king solidified loyalties.

4.9. External Relations and Military Actions

Though the scale of Egyptian imperialism seen in later kingdoms had not yet begun, there were signs of external relations during the Early Dynastic Period:

- **Nubia**: Egyptian expeditions may have reached into Lower Nubia to gain gold, cattle, and other resources. The boundary likely moved back and forth, with fortifications established in some regions.
- **Libyan Desert**: Nomadic tribes might have posed occasional threats to western borders, leading to small campaigns or defensive measures.
- **Sinai**: Expeditions to mine **copper** and **turquoise** in Sinai seem to date back to at least the Early Dynastic Period. Royal inscriptions on rocks in the Sinai mention the presence of the Egyptian court.
- **Levant**: Trade connections brought influences from Canaan or beyond, though large-scale military campaigns in the Levant are not well documented this early.

While we do not see major conquest records from Dynasties 1 and 2, the presence of Egyptian artifacts in neighboring lands, and vice versa, shows that diplomacy or controlled interactions were important.

4.10. Key Rulers of the First Dynasty

The First Dynasty typically includes the following kings (though spellings vary):

1. **Narmer (possibly Menes)**: Credited with unification.
2. **Hor-Aha**: May have continued Narmer's policies, built temples, and possibly expanded Memphis.
3. **Djer**: Notable for a large tomb at Abydos; numerous grave goods discovered.
4. **Djet** (sometimes spelled Wadj): Known for stelae bearing his name, found at Abydos.
5. **Den**: Introduced some innovations, including the first depiction of the **Double Crown** on a relief. He was a powerful ruler who left behind a well-furnished tomb.
6. **Anedjib**, **Semerkhet**, and **Qa'a**: The final rulers of the First Dynasty, though details about their reigns are less certain.

Each king left behind unique tombs or stelae. Over this century or so, **royal institutions** solidified, the role of the pharaoh became better defined, and the kingdom's administration grew more sophisticated.

4.11. Second Dynasty Developments

The Second Dynasty continued many First Dynasty traditions but also saw some conflicts or shifts:

- **Raneb**, **Nynetjer**, and **Weneg**: Early Second Dynasty rulers who maintained power at Memphis but may have faced internal challenges.
- **Sened**: Possibly reigned during a period when the Delta had some form of rival leadership—scholars debate the evidence.
- **Peribsen**: A notable king whose **Serekh** (the royal crest) replaced the falcon (Horus) with the **Seth animal**, suggesting internal religious or political changes. This caused speculation about a rift in religious or political unity.
- **Khasekhemwy**: The last ruler of the Second Dynasty, he restored some form of national stability. His name incorporates both **Horus** and **Seth**, implying a reconciliation of religious factions or political camps.

By the end of the Second Dynasty, Egypt was again firmly unified. The successes and failures of these early rulers paved the way for the **Third Dynasty** and the dawn of the Old Kingdom, where stone pyramid building would emerge.

4.12. Religious Evolution

During Dynasties 1 and 2, the **concept of the afterlife** and **religious practices** became more elaborate:

- **Offering formulas** may have developed, in which the king or an elite person requests offerings from various gods.
- **Royal enclosures** (like those at Abydos for King Khasekhemwy) might have served ceremonial or religious functions tied to the king's role as a living god.
- **Cult of the King**: Officials began building shrines or stelae dedicated to the king's cult. After a ruler's death, continuing rites honored him as an eternal caretaker of the land.

These religious innovations created a more formal link between the monarchy and the gods, reinforcing the concept that the pharaoh's authority was sacred.

4.13. Advances in Writing and Administration

In Chapter 3, we saw the earliest proto-writing in the late Predynastic. By the Early Dynastic Period:

1. **Hieroglyphics**: The system became more standardized. Carvings on palace walls, tomb stelae, and royal labels used pictures for sounds and ideas.
2. **Hieratic**: A cursive form developed for everyday writing on papyrus, easier than carving full hieroglyphs. Although few papyrus documents survive from this era, later evidence suggests it existed in some form.
3. **Seals and labels**: Officials used cylinder seals or stamp seals to mark containers. The impression contained the name of the king or the office, ensuring authenticity.
4. **Accounting**: Records of harvest yields, livestock counts, and workforce allocations hint at a more sophisticated economy.

These developments in writing and administration were essential for running a complex state. They made it possible to manage resources on a national scale, a major step up from the smaller chiefdoms of the Predynastic.

4.14. Social Stratification

By the Early Dynastic Period, Egyptian society had multiple layers:

- **The King (Pharaoh)**: At the very top, seen as both mortal ruler and divine being.
- **Royal Family and High Officials**: Princes, princesses, and high-ranked administrators like the **Vizier**.
- **Priests**: In charge of religious rites, temple upkeep, and theological matters. Priestly roles became more defined as state religion took hold.
- **Scribes**: Essential for administration, documenting everything from land measurements to religious texts.
- **Artisans and Craftsmen**: Stone carvers, metalworkers, potters, weavers, and builders who supplied the court and temple with specialized goods.
- **Farmers**: The vast majority of the population, working the land to produce grain and other crops. They provided the economic base of the state.
- **Servants and Possibly Slaves**: Those who labored under direct authority for temples, the royal household, or powerful nobles. Evidence of slavery is limited for this period, but forms of bonded labor likely existed.

This hierarchy allowed the monarchy to direct massive labor forces when needed, as seen in the construction of royal tombs. In return, the king was expected to maintain **ma'at**—the cosmic order of balance, justice, and prosperity.

4.15. Daily Life in the Early Dynastic Period

While the king and nobles left the most tangible records in tombs and monuments, ordinary people led simpler lives:

- **Housing**: Mudbrick houses with minimal rooms, sometimes two stories for wealthier families. The interior included a main living space, a storage area, and a roof used for sleeping during hot nights.
- **Food and Drink**: Bread and beer formed the staples. People also ate onions, garlic, lettuce, beans, lentils, fish, and occasionally meat.

- **Clothing**: Linen kilts or shifts, with heavier wraps in cooler months. Women might have worn straight dresses with straps, while men typically wore kilts.
- **Leisure and Pastimes**: Games (like **Senet**, though it becomes more documented later), music with simple instruments (harps or flutes), and storytelling by oral tradition.
- **Local Rituals**: Families practiced small-scale worship at household altars, likely offering bread, beer, or incense to gods or ancestors.

4.16. Artifacts and Cultural Expressions

Several distinctive artifacts give us insight into Early Dynastic culture:

- **Stone Vessels**: Created in a variety of shapes from hard stones like alabaster or diorite. The skill required shows advanced craftsmanship.
- **Maceheads**: Ceremonial weapons, often carved with relief scenes of the king in triumphant or religious poses.
- **Labels and Tags**: Small ivory or wooden tags tied to goods, inscribed with the king's name or a short text describing content or origin.
- **Stelae**: Upright stone slabs bearing the name of the deceased or the king, marking tombs or other significant sites.

Collectively, these objects reveal a people invested in orderly administration, religious rites, and the demonstration of royal power.

4.17. Shifts in Religious Centers

Though Memphis held administrative power, other cities retained or gained religious significance:

- **Heliopolis** (near modern Cairo) was associated with the sun god Re.
- **Butic** or **Pe** in the Delta was linked to the worship of the cobra goddess Wadjet.
- **Nekhbet** in Upper Egypt was symbolized by the vulture goddess Nekhbet.

The idea of "Two Ladies" (Nekhbet for Upper Egypt and Wadjet for Lower Egypt) merged under the king's regalia, showing religious unification as well as political. Each region brought its local deities into a wider pantheon that the king presided over, ensuring that no major deity was left out of the official state cult.

4.18. Challenges and Conflicts

Not everything was smooth in Dynasties 1 and 2. There is evidence of:

- **Brief Internal Divisions**: Possibly in the Second Dynasty when the Seth worship under King Peribsen contrasted the established Horus tradition.
- **Rebellions or Local Disputes**: The unification was still new, and local leaders might have tested the king's authority.
- **Succession Issues**: The order of the Second Dynasty kings and their relationships are not fully clear, suggesting potential power struggles or contested successions.

Despite these issues, the Early Dynastic Period ended with a kingdom still intact, poised for the next major era of innovation and monumental architecture: the Old Kingdom.

4.19. Legacy of the Early Dynasties

The Early Dynastic Period laid critical foundations:

1. **Political and Administrative**: A centralized government with the pharaoh at its head and an evolving bureaucracy beneath him.
2. **Religious**: The concept of divine kingship, with the king's role as Horus on Earth, was firmly established.
3. **Cultural**: Artistic conventions (frontal poses, stylized relief scenes) and architectural forms (mastaba tombs, palace façades) influenced later periods.
4. **Economic**: Systematic collection of surplus, resource redistribution, and expanded trade networks that would support massive building projects in the centuries to come.

By the end of the Second Dynasty, Egypt was no longer a patchwork of local cultures. Instead, it was a unified kingdom with shared beliefs, a budding bureaucracy, and royal families that commanded respect and resources on a scale unprecedented in earlier times.

CHAPTER 5

THE OLD KINGDOM

5.1. Introduction to the Old Kingdom

The **Old Kingdom** spans roughly from **2686 to 2181 BCE** and covers the **Third Dynasty** through the **Sixth Dynasty**, though some sources include later dynasties in the definition. This era is often called the "Age of the Pyramids," because it was during these centuries that Egyptian pharaohs directed the building of massive pyramid complexes. These monuments have survived thousands of years and remain among the greatest architectural achievements in human history.

The Old Kingdom was also a time of centralization and strong royal power. The pharaoh was seen not only as the political head of the nation but also as a divine or semi-divine figure responsible for maintaining the cosmic balance called **ma'at**. A complex government structure developed under the king, enabling large-scale building projects and economic planning. Art styles matured, religious beliefs expanded, and Egypt began to interact more with neighboring regions. By the end of the Old Kingdom, however, power struggles and administrative issues led to a decline in central authority, setting the stage for the First Intermediate Period.

5.2. The Rise of the Third Dynasty

After the Early Dynastic Period (First and Second Dynasties), the **Third Dynasty** (c. 2686–2613 BCE) marked the formal start of the Old Kingdom. The first king commonly recognized for this period is **Djoser**. There may have been other short-lived rulers before him, but our evidence is fragmentary. Under the Third Dynasty, Memphis remained the capital and an important administrative center.

During this dynasty, we see the continued use of **mastaba** tombs for high officials and some early attempts at more ambitious royal monuments. The shift from mudbrick to stone construction also became more pronounced, as building in stone reflected the king's grand vision and desire for permanence.

5.3. King Djoser and His Achievements

Djoser is the most famous Third Dynasty pharaoh. He reigned for perhaps two decades or more. A few key highlights of his reign include:

1. **Administrative Growth**: Djoser strengthened the state bureaucracy by appointing capable officials to oversee the collection of taxes, distribution of resources, and recruitment of labor for construction.
2. **Religious Consolidation**: He promoted the royal cult, presenting himself as a divine intermediary who maintained ma'at in Egypt. Temples dedicated to local gods continued to receive support from the state, and the king's own divine status further unified the country.
3. **Economic Management**: By keeping track of harvests, livestock, and craft production, the king could plan large building projects and guarantee food rations for laborers.

Djoser's most enduring legacy, however, is his massive building project at **Saqqara**, near Memphis.

5.4. Imhotep and the Step Pyramid

During Djoser's reign, an official named **Imhotep** became the king's chief architect and is often credited with designing the **Step Pyramid Complex** at Saqqara. Imhotep was a man of many talents—an architect, high priest, doctor, and advisor to the king. He later became deified in Egyptian tradition as a patron of wisdom and medicine.

5.4.1. Transition from Mastaba to Pyramid

Before Djoser's time, royal burials used mastabas—rectangular mudbrick structures with flat roofs. Imhotep's breakthrough was stacking several mastaba-like layers on top of one another to form a **step pyramid**. This structure rose in a series of terraces, each one smaller than the layer below, creating a stepped shape. The Step Pyramid is:

- **Constructed in Stone**: While earlier mastabas sometimes used stone blocks for facing, the Step Pyramid was the first large-scale monument built almost entirely in stone.
- **Complex Surrounding Architecture**: The pyramid was part of a broader ceremonial complex that included courtyards, temples, shrines, and a

protective wall. These spaces likely hosted rituals to honor the king and the gods.
- **Symbol of Divine Power**: By creating such an imposing, enduring monument, Djoser demonstrated his godlike status and proclaimed his role as protector of Egypt.

The Step Pyramid of Djoser stands about 60 meters tall. It was the tallest structure of its time and the first monumental stone building in history. This innovation laid the foundation for the grand pyramid-building tradition that followed in the Fourth Dynasty.

5.5. The Fourth Dynasty and the Great Pyramids

The **Fourth Dynasty** (c. 2613–2494 BCE) represents the high point of the Old Kingdom pyramid-building era. The most famous pharaohs of this period are **Sneferu, Khufu, Khafre,** and **Menkaure**. Their names are forever linked to the enormous pyramids they built, particularly on the Giza Plateau.

5.5.1. Sneferu's Contributions

Sneferu, the first king of the Fourth Dynasty, is sometimes called the "greatest pyramid builder" due to the sheer scale of his construction projects. He is credited with building at least three major pyramids:

1. **Meidum Pyramid**: Begun under the last Third Dynasty king (possibly Huni) and completed or modified by Sneferu. At some point, it suffered a collapse of its outer layers, leaving a tall tower-like structure.
2. **Bent Pyramid** at Dahshur: This pyramid starts with steep angles that suddenly change midway, giving it a bent appearance. Scholars debate whether this was due to structural concerns or a design change mid-construction.
3. **Red Pyramid** at Dahshur: Considered the first true smooth-sided pyramid. It is called the "Red Pyramid" because of the reddish hue of its limestone blocks.

These constructions show trial and error in pyramid design, as architects learned how to manage weight, angles, and internal chambers. By the end of Sneferu's reign, builders had perfected the art of constructing a true pyramid shape.

5.5.2. Khufu and the Great Pyramid

Khufu (sometimes called Cheops by the Greeks) was Sneferu's son and the builder of the **Great Pyramid at Giza**, one of the Seven Wonders of the Ancient World. Standing about 146 meters tall when completed, the Great Pyramid remained the world's tallest man-made structure for over 3,800 years.

Key points about the Great Pyramid:

- **Precision**: The base is nearly a perfect square, with sides oriented almost exactly to the cardinal points (north, south, east, west).
- **Massive Labor Force**: Modern estimates suggest tens of thousands of workers. They were likely peasant farmers conscripted during the Nile's flood season when fields were not being worked. Skilled craftsmen and engineers oversaw the shaping, transporting, and placing of massive limestone and granite blocks.
- **Interior Layout**: The pyramid contains multiple chambers and passageways, including the King's Chamber, Queen's Chamber, and a mysterious "Grand Gallery." How the Egyptians engineered these internal structures without modern tools remains a subject of study and fascination.
- **Purpose**: Like other pyramids, it was a tomb for the king. But it also served as a cosmic symbol, representing a place of rebirth and ascension for the pharaoh's soul.

Khufu's reign is often associated with absolute central power. Ancient Greek historian Herodotus wrote stories—likely exaggerated—about Khufu's harsh rule. Actual evidence from the period is sparse, but the sheer scale of the Great Pyramid suggests significant organization and resources at the king's disposal.

5.5.3. Khafre, Menkaure, and the Sphinx

Khufu's successors continued building on the Giza plateau:

- **Khafre (Chephren)**: Erected the second-largest pyramid at Giza. This pyramid appears taller from some viewpoints because it stands on higher ground. The famous **Great Sphinx**—carved from the bedrock—likely dates to Khafre's reign. The Sphinx has the body of a lion and a human head, possibly bearing Khafre's likeness, symbolizing the king's power and divine authority.

- **Menkaure (Mycerinus)**: Built the smallest of the three main Giza pyramids. Though not as large as his father's or grandfather's, Menkaure's pyramid shows continued commitment to the royal building tradition. The detail in the surrounding mortuary temples and the quality of sculpture from his reign are notable.

The Giza complex is an enduring symbol of Egyptian civilization. Each pyramid was part of a larger funerary complex containing temples, causeways, and subsidiary pyramids or tombs for royal family members.

5.6. Society, Economy, and Administration During the Old Kingdom

5.6.1. Central Bureaucracy

To build and maintain pyramids, pharaohs required a **well-structured government**. Key officials included:

- **Vizier**: The highest official under the king, often a royal relative. The vizier oversaw the treasury, agriculture, legal matters, and royal building projects.
- **Nomarchs**: Governors of provinces called "nomes." Each nome had its local temple cults, officials, and scribes. Nomarchs collected taxes and sent resources to the king.
- **Scribes**: Essential to record-keeping. They tallied grain, drafted orders, organized labor, and kept track of the workforce.

The scale of the pyramid projects also required specialized labor: **engineers**, **architects**, **stonecutters**, **transport organizers**, and **artisans**. Managing thousands of workers showed remarkable administrative skill.

5.6.2. Agricultural Base

The **Nile's flood cycle** provided fertile soil for wheat, barley, flax, and other crops. Farmers were taxed in grain, which the state stored in granaries. This surplus allowed the government to feed the labor force building pyramids. Some people mistakenly believe that slaves built the pyramids, but most modern scholars think they were workers conscripted during the off-season from farming. Many were well-fed, given housing, and organized into teams. Skilled laborers and foremen received better accommodation and compensation.

5.6.3. Trade and Expeditions

During the Old Kingdom, Egyptians undertook **expeditions** to obtain exotic goods and raw materials:

- **Nubia (to the south)**: Source of gold, ebony, ivory, and other luxury goods.
- **Sinai Peninsula**: Rich in copper and turquoise.
- **Byblos (in modern Lebanon)**: Supplied cedar wood, used for shipbuilding and large construction beams.
- **Western Desert Oases**: Provided additional resources like salt and certain minerals.

These trade connections enriched the royal court and fueled the building programs. While not an era of aggressive military conquest, the Old Kingdom pharaohs did secure trade routes and sometimes built forts or outposts to protect caravans.

5.7. Art and Culture in the Old Kingdom

Art in the Old Kingdom reached a level of sophistication that influenced later periods. The hallmark of this era's art is a focus on **order, symmetry, and idealized forms**.

5.7.1. Sculptural Advances

- **Royal Statues**: Kings were depicted in a perfect, almost godlike form. The statue of Khafre enthroned, carved in diorite, is a prime example. It shows the king seated calmly, with the falcon of Horus protectively behind his head.
- **Private Tomb Sculptures**: Nobles commissioned statues of themselves and their families. One famous example is the painted limestone statue known as the "Seated Scribe," which shows a less idealized and more realistic portrayal, offering insight into non-royal portraiture.

5.7.2. Relief Carvings and Tomb Decoration

Wealthy courtiers decorated their mastaba tombs with **painted reliefs** that illustrated daily life—farming, fishing, hunting, crafts, and family gatherings. These scenes reveal much about Old Kingdom society, showing the roles of men and women, types of food production, and cultural practices.

Tomb inscriptions also grew more detailed, listing titles of the deceased and prayers for offerings. Over time, these developed into the **"Offering Formula,"** requesting bread, beer, cattle, and fowl for the spirit.

5.7.3. Religious Changes

Religion in the Old Kingdom emphasized the divine role of the pharaoh. But worship of other deities also expanded:

- **Ra (Re)**, the sun god of Heliopolis, became increasingly important. Kings were called "Sons of Re," cementing the link between solar worship and royal authority.
- **Pyramid Texts**: By the end of the Old Kingdom (Fifth and Sixth Dynasties), parts of the internal pyramid walls were inscribed with religious spells to guide the king's soul in the afterlife. These are among the oldest known religious texts in Egypt, forming the basis of later "Coffin Texts" and "Book of the Dead."

5.8. The Fifth Dynasty: Emphasis on Sun Cult

The **Fifth Dynasty** (c. 2494–2345 BCE) saw a shift toward more emphasis on the **sun god Re**. Some noteworthy kings from this dynasty include **Userkaf, Sahure, Neferirkare Kakai, Shepseskare, Neferefre**, and **Nyuserre Ini**.

- **Sun Temples**: These kings built special temples dedicated to Re in the area of Abusir, south of Giza. The temples often included a large obelisk-like structure (called a ben-ben stone) in an open courtyard where rituals to the sun god took place.
- **Changes in Pyramid Size**: While these rulers still built pyramids, many were smaller than those of the Fourth Dynasty. The focus of architecture began to shift from the size of the pyramid to the complexity of the surrounding temple complexes.
- **Relief Scenes**: The relief decorations in the mortuary temples and sun temples grew in detail and quality. Scenes of the king interacting with the gods, or of state activities like trade expeditions and ceremonies, are carved in fine limestone.

Religion continued to evolve, placing the king firmly in a solar framework. The pharaoh was seen as the living son of Re, and each day's sunrise reinforced the notion of royal authority.

5.9. Administration and Nobility During the Fifth Dynasty

Noble families grew more influential during the Fifth Dynasty. Many high officials, who held important titles like **Vizier**, also had close ties to the royal family. Large tombs at Saqqara and Abusir show the rising wealth of these officials. Inscriptions tell us about:

- **Duties of Officials**: Overseeing royal estates, temples, and building projects.
- **Royal Decrees**: The king might grant land or tax exemptions to temples and loyal nobles, written on stone stelae or papyrus.
- **Craft Workshops**: Workshops connected to the temples or palaces produced fine goods for the court and for trade or diplomatic gifts.

The growth of noble power had a significant effect on the later part of the Old Kingdom, as local governors (nomarchs) and priests started gaining wealth and authority in their regions.

5.10. The Sixth Dynasty: Peak and Decline

The **Sixth Dynasty** (c. 2345–2181 BCE) is often seen as the final part of the Old Kingdom. Early rulers like **Teti** and **Userkare** continued the traditions of the Fifth Dynasty. However, two reigns stand out:

1. **Pepi I**: His pyramid complex at Saqqara included elaborate reliefs, and he expanded trade contacts. Under Pepi I, officials became increasingly powerful in provincial areas.
2. **Pepi II**: Traditionally said to have ruled over 90 years (some doubt that figure, but it was still a very long reign). By the end of Pepi II's rule, central power had weakened. Nomarchs in various nomes held semi-autonomous power, building large tombs in their own districts, which rivaled royal constructions.

This loss of centralized control, along with possible low Nile floods, economic strain, and political rivalries, contributed to the breakdown of the Old Kingdom at the end of the Sixth Dynasty.

5.11. Women's Roles in the Old Kingdom

While men dominated the highest ranks of government, **women** in the Old Kingdom could still hold positions of influence, especially if they were linked to the royal family. Some queens and royal mothers acted as regents for young kings, though evidence is sparse. Elite women also served as priestesses of goddesses like **Hathor** or **Neith**, and a few carried titles suggesting that they managed estates or temple holdings.

The art of the period sometimes shows women involved in daily life—managing household activities or participating in estate matters. Though the king's mother and principal wife were highly respected, the notion of a ruling queen was very rare in the Old Kingdom.

5.12. Foreign Relations and Expeditions

Most Old Kingdom rulers focused on internal affairs and building projects, but there were important foreign interactions:

- **Nubia**: Egyptians established trading posts or small forts along the Nile south of Aswan to control resources like gold, hardwood, incense, and animal products.
- **Punt**: Expeditions to the land of Punt (likely in the Horn of Africa region) may have started by the late Fifth or Sixth Dynasty, though evidence is better documented in later periods. Punt supplied incense, myrrh, and exotic goods.
- **Libya and Western Desert**: Egyptian influence in these areas included trade or occasional military forays. The desert oases provided resources and routes for caravans.
- **Syria-Palestine**: Some Old Kingdom reliefs mention trade with or expeditions to the Levant, acquiring cedar wood, wine, and other foreign products. Military actions here are not well-documented in the Old Kingdom, though there could have been small-scale raids or defensive measures.

No large territorial empire was created in the Old Kingdom, unlike in the New Kingdom centuries later. Instead, foreign relations aimed at securing valuable materials and exotic luxuries for the royal court and temples.

5.13. Religious Life of Ordinary People

Although the king's relationship to the gods was central, local temples and household altars existed. Commoners prayed to deities for protection, health, and fertility. Small clay figurines or amulets might represent protective gods or animals. The average person believed that living a righteous life, following ma'at, was essential.

Burials for commoners were simpler than the elaborate tombs of the elites. Bodies were often placed in shallow graves or small mastabas if the family could afford it. Grave goods were minimal—ceramic vessels, a few personal items, or amulets. Nonetheless, these practices show a belief in some form of afterlife accessible to ordinary people, though not as grand as the royal hereafter.

5.14. Literature and Written Records

Written texts from the Old Kingdom are somewhat limited. We have:

- **Royal Decrees and Inscriptions**: Typically announcing temple endowments or appointments of officials.
- **Tomb Autobiographies**: High officials sometimes included carved "autobiographical texts" in their tomb chapels, praising their deeds, loyalty to the king, and moral conduct.
- **Pyramid Texts**: Inside the pyramids of later Fifth Dynasty and Sixth Dynasty kings, we find spells and recitations intended to guide the king's spirit in the afterlife.

Longer literary works, like the **Instruction Texts** (didactic teachings) and **Wisdom Literature**, appear more fully in the Middle Kingdom, though their roots may lie in the Old Kingdom's oral traditions.

5.15. Artisans and Construction Techniques

The building of pyramids and temples required advanced technical knowledge. Egyptians understood how to quarry large stone blocks, transport them by boat on the Nile, and move them overland using sledges and rollers. Workers used copper chisels, stone pounders, wooden levers, and rope systems to shape and move blocks. Skilled stonemasons could achieve smooth finishes and precise alignments.

Artisans who specialized in relief carving, sculpture, pottery, and jewelry enjoyed a respected position, as the royal family and nobility demanded high-quality items. The workshop areas discovered at pyramid sites reveal systematic organization of labor, with specialized teams working on stone, wood, or metal.

5.16. The Decline of the Old Kingdom

By the later Sixth Dynasty, several factors contributed to instability:

1. **Long Reign of Pepi II**: If he indeed ruled over 90 years, the government might have become rigid or prone to internal rivalries, especially after the king aged.
2. **Growing Power of Nomarchs**: Regional governors amassed wealth and influence, sometimes challenging or ignoring the central government's authority. They built their own tombs and controlled local labor, weakening the king's monopoly on resources.
3. **Economic Strains**: Funding massive tombs and temples over generations may have strained resources, especially if the Nile floods were inadequate or trade declined.
4. **Possible Climate Changes**: Some scholars suggest that lower Nile floods or broader climate shifts contributed to famines or unrest.

By **2181 BCE**, central rule fragmented. The seat of the pharaoh lost much of its power, ushering in a period of division known as the **First Intermediate Period**.

5.17. Achievements and Legacy

Despite its eventual decline, the Old Kingdom remains a pinnacle of ancient Egyptian achievement:

- **Architectural Marvels**: The pyramids at Giza, the Step Pyramid at Saqqara, and other monuments still stand as wonders of engineering.
- **Artistic Canon**: Old Kingdom art established the proportions and style that would define Egyptian art for centuries.
- **Religious Foundation**: The concept of the divinized king, the solar cult, and the development of funerary texts shaped later beliefs and practices.
- **Administrative Model**: The centralized government, though it eventually weakened, served as a template for future dynasties.

This epoch profoundly influenced how later Egyptians viewed their past. They saw the Old Kingdom as a golden age, even if it ended in political fragmentation. In the next chapter, we turn to the **First Intermediate Period**, when Egypt found itself divided between competing power centers. Only after much struggle would a new line of kings reunite the land and usher in the Middle Kingdom.

CHAPTER 6

THE FIRST INTERMEDIATE PERIOD

6.1. Introduction to the First Intermediate Period

The **First Intermediate Period** (c. 2181–2055 BCE) follows the collapse of the Old Kingdom and precedes the Middle Kingdom. It was a time when central authority broke down, and **regional leaders** (nomarchs) gained power. Many texts from later periods portray these years as chaotic and full of hardships such as famine, lawlessness, and social upheaval. While some accounts may be exaggerated, there is evidence that the state's organization faltered, leading to rival rulers in different parts of the country.

The First Intermediate Period covers roughly the **Seventh, Eighth, Ninth, Tenth,** and part of the **Eleventh Dynasties**—though the numbering and sequence of rulers can be confusing, since written records from this era are scarce or fragmentary. Ultimately, a family of rulers from **Thebes** in Upper Egypt reunited the land, laying the foundation for the Middle Kingdom.

6.2. The Collapse of Central Authority

In the final decades of the Old Kingdom, the government's power weakened. Several factors contributed to this collapse:

1. **Political Fragmentation**: After Pepi II's very long reign, a clear line of succession became murky. Minor or short-lived kings followed, each failing to solidify strong central control.
2. **Economic Problems**: The massive expenses of pyramid building and temple endowments may have drained the royal treasury. In addition, climate changes or low Nile floods led to poor harvests.
3. **Rise of the Nomarchs**: Provincial governors (nomarchs) had grown wealthy and autonomous, especially in Upper Egypt. Some maintained local armies or alliances separate from the king's authority.
4. **Possible Social Unrest**: Tomb autobiographies and later texts hint at robberies, local feuds, and a breakdown of law and order in certain areas.

As a result, the country splintered into smaller power centers. In Lower Egypt, a line of short-lived kings tried to maintain the throne at Memphis but lacked real authority. In Middle and Upper Egypt, local rulers began to assert independence, controlling their nomes like mini-kingdoms.

6.3. The Seventh and Eighth Dynasties: Phantom Kings

Egyptian king lists mention the **Seventh and Eighth Dynasties** as direct successors to the Sixth Dynasty at Memphis, but very little is known about them. The **Seventh Dynasty** is described by some ancient sources as having 70 kings in 70 days—likely a satire implying many weak rulers in quick succession.

The **Eighth Dynasty** also appears short-lived. A few names, such as **Neferkare II** or **Neferkare Neby**, appear in later records, but their reigns probably spanned only a few months or years. These dynasties failed to restore unity, and the seat of power effectively moved away from Memphis.

6.4. Herakleopolitan Kings (Ninth and Tenth Dynasties)

By around **2160 BCE**, a new center of power emerged at **Herakleopolis Magna**, located in **Middle Egypt** (south of the Faiyum region). Rulers from Herakleopolis formed the **Ninth and Tenth Dynasties**. The founder is sometimes listed as **Khety I** or **Akhtoy I**.

6.4.1. Policies and Governance

The Herakleopolitan kings tried to restore order over Lower Egypt and parts of Middle Egypt. They sent officials to oversee nomes, introduced some administrative reforms, and may have revived certain Old Kingdom traditions. However, they did not control Upper Egypt fully, where local rulers in Thebes were rising.

Despite limited records, it seems that under the stronger Herakleopolitan kings, the delta and Middle Egypt saw some stability. Tomb inscriptions in the region mention efforts to maintain irrigation, distribute grain, and hold local councils.

6.4.2. Cultural and Religious Life

While there was no return to massive pyramid building, local nobles and kings still constructed modest tombs. Art became more regionally varied, reflecting local tastes rather than a single royal style. Religion remained important, though no single king could fund large temple projects as the Old Kingdom pharaohs did. Provincial cults thrived, giving each region a stronger sense of identity.

6.5. The Rise of Thebes

In **Upper Egypt**, the city of **Thebes** (modern Luxor) developed into a powerful rival to Herakleopolis. The local rulers there began claiming titles like "Overseer of Upper Egypt" or even "King," depending on their ambitions. The **Eleventh Dynasty** traces its origins to these Theban nomarchs. Over time, Theban rulers such as **Intef I**, **Intef II**, and **Intef III** expanded their control northward, clashing with the Herakleopolitan kings.

6.6. Role of Local Nomarchs

Throughout the First Intermediate Period, the **nomarchs** held significant power. Instead of sending all their surplus to a distant king, they used it to fortify their nomes, build local tombs, and sponsor local religious festivals. Some nomarchs ruled their territories almost like small independent states.

Prominent examples include:

- The **nomes of Asyut**, which were strategically located and sometimes shifted alliances between north and south.
- The **nomes around Abydos**, where local leaders might have capitalized on the region's religious importance.

This fragmentation of authority meant that alliances, marriages, and occasional warfare between nomes shaped the political map. In many ways, the First Intermediate Period resembles a feudal structure where local lords held real power.

6.7. Social Changes

Evidence suggests that during the First Intermediate Period, more opportunities arose for individuals outside the traditional elite circles. In some tomb inscriptions, non-royal people claimed titles once reserved for higher nobility. Funerary objects also became more widespread, with middle-class individuals gaining access to decorated coffins or tomb reliefs.

At the same time, literature from later eras refers to chaos, describing how "the poor man becomes rich" and "the rich man loses everything." These references may be exaggerated, but they do point to a shift in social norms or a feeling of upheaval as older hierarchies changed and local power structures replaced the monarchy's central authority.

6.8. Art and Architecture in the First Intermediate Period

Art styles during this period are less uniform than in the Old Kingdom. Since there was no strong central court to dictate artistic standards, regional approaches flourished:

1. **Tomb Decorations**: Some tombs in Upper Egypt show lively, more simplified relief styles. Artists used brighter colors and sometimes less precise proportions than seen in Old Kingdom works.
2. **Funerary Stelae**: Many local officials erected stelae inscribed with autobiographical texts praising their leadership, generosity, or devotion to local gods.
3. **Coffin Texts**: Spell collections, derived from earlier Pyramid Texts, began appearing on the insides of coffins. They offered prayers and protection for the deceased, indicating that afterlife beliefs were spreading beyond royalty.

Architecture focused more on local needs—such as building small temples or strengthening city walls—than on grand national monuments.

6.9. Religious Continuity and Local Deities

Despite political fragmentation, fundamental Egyptian religious ideas carried on. The concept of **ma'at** endured, though each local ruler claimed to uphold it. Worship of traditional gods like **Re**, **Osiris**, **Hathor**, and **Amun** continued in different areas. Thebes, for instance, emphasized the worship of **Amun**, who would rise to prominence in later dynasties.

During this period, the **Osiris cult** seems to have grown stronger, focusing on personal salvation and the hope of eternal life. Texts mentioning Osiris as the ruler of the underworld became more common, reflecting an increasing democratization of afterlife beliefs.

6.10. Warfare, Diplomacy, and Shifting Alliances

The Herakleopolitan kings faced challenges in maintaining control over Middle Egypt. The Theban rulers in the south gradually marched north, winning over or subduing local nomarchs. Some nomarchs allied with Thebes, hoping for better prospects under a new regime; others stayed loyal to Herakleopolis for as long as possible.

Sporadic conflicts flared along the border regions between the territories controlled by Herakleopolis and Thebes. These battles sometimes resulted in pillaging or destruction of rival districts. Local leaders might also shift allegiances if the situation turned in favor of one side.

6.11. The Tension Between Herakleopolis and Thebes

By the mid-First Intermediate Period, Egypt was effectively split into at least two main zones:

1. **Herakleopolitan Kingdom (Ninth and Tenth Dynasties)**: Controlling the northern nomes and parts of Middle Egypt.
2. **Theban Kingdom (Eleventh Dynasty beginnings)**: Dominating Upper Egypt and pushing northward.

Each side sought to unify Egypt under its leadership, but the Theban forces gradually gained the upper hand. Royal inscriptions from the Theban Intef rulers proudly list their victories, capturing towns once loyal to Herakleopolis. Over time, it became clear that Thebes would likely prevail in the struggle for national dominance.

6.12. Attempts at Reunification

The first strong Theban rulers were the **Intefs**: **Intef I**, **Intef II**, and **Intef III**. They took the title of "**King**" and started building more elaborate tomb complexes near Thebes. **Intef II** expanded Theban influence as far north as Abydos, challenging Herakleopolitan rule. By the time of **Intef III**, Thebes was a significant regional power.

These wars were not continuous large-scale campaigns but rather a series of skirmishes, negotiations, and alliances. Thebes slowly absorbed nearby nomes, moving the border of their domain further north. The Herakleopolitan kings struggled to keep the loyalty of Middle Egypt, facing desertions from local nobles who turned southward, possibly seeing Thebes as more stable or more powerful.

6.13. The Emergence of Mentuhotep II

The Theban ruler who finally succeeded in reuniting Egypt was **Mentuhotep II** (also known as **Nebhepetre Mentuhotep**). He was likely the son or grandson of Intef III, and he came to the throne around **2060 BCE**. Early in his reign, he continued the campaign against the last Herakleopolitan kings. After a series of battles, Herakleopolis fell, and Mentuhotep II declared himself the king of a fully unified Egypt around **c. 2055 BCE**.

With this victory, Mentuhotep II founded what scholars call the **Middle Kingdom** (usually counted as the later part of the Eleventh Dynasty through the Twelfth Dynasty, and sometimes the Thirteenth). Mentuhotep II based his rule in Thebes, but he likely restored Memphis as an important administrative center, balancing the old traditions with new power structures.

6.14. Cultural and Political Shifts Under Mentuhotep II

Once Mentuhotep II established control, he began reforms to stabilize Egypt:

- **Government Reorganization**: He reinstated a centralized administration, likely appointing loyal supporters as nomarchs or limiting the power of local rulers. Some families kept their positions if they pledged loyalty to the new king.
- **Monumental Construction**: Mentuhotep II built a unique funerary temple at Deir el-Bahari, near Thebes. This complex integrated a temple facade with the natural cliffs, highlighting Thebes' growing religious status.
- **Propaganda and Legitimacy**: The new regime emphasized that Mentuhotep II had restored ma'at, ending the "chaos" of the First Intermediate Period. In official inscriptions, he is hailed as a unifier and restorer of prosperity.

These changes mark the birth of a renewed sense of national identity. The long period of division had ended. Under Mentuhotep II and his successors, Egypt would enjoy a rebirth of centralized power, leading to the Middle Kingdom's achievements.

6.15. Legacy of the First Intermediate Period

While often depicted as a dark age, the First Intermediate Period also had lasting effects:

1. **Rise of Thebes**: This city became a major religious and political center for centuries to come, primarily due to the success of its ruling dynasty.
2. **Local Culture**: Art styles, administrative practices, and religious traditions in the provinces developed independently, leading to a more diverse cultural landscape when the country was reunited.
3. **Expanded Afterlife Beliefs**: The distribution of Coffin Texts and the idea that non-royal individuals could partake in a blessed afterlife began to spread more widely, setting a pattern for Middle Kingdom religion.
4. **Lesson in Governance**: Later pharaohs recognized that a too-powerful aristocracy and lack of strong succession plans could destabilize the kingdom.

6.16. Looking Ahead to the Middle Kingdom

The First Intermediate Period was turbulent, but it paved the way for the **Middle Kingdom**, which many historians label as a classical age of Egyptian culture. The reorganization of government, the blending of local and royal traditions, and the expansion of religious thought all contributed to the new era. In the Middle Kingdom, pharaohs would rule more flexibly, forging closer ties with provincial elites to maintain unity.

CHAPTER 7

THE MIDDLE KINGDOM

7.1. Overview of the Middle Kingdom

The **Middle Kingdom** traditionally spans the **late Eleventh Dynasty** through the **Twelfth Dynasty** and sometimes includes parts of the **Thirteenth Dynasty**, covering roughly **2055 to 1650 BCE**. Egyptologists often describe it as a second "classical age" of ancient Egyptian civilization, comparable in its cultural achievements to the Old Kingdom pyramid age. Yet, the Middle Kingdom was unique because it emerged from a period of disunity (the First Intermediate Period) and saw the rapid rebuilding of state power, the strengthening of royal authority, and an outpouring of cultural and literary creativity.

During the Middle Kingdom, the city of **Thebes** rose to national prominence, especially under the Eleventh Dynasty rulers who reunified the country. Later, the royal court shifted its center of power northward under the Twelfth Dynasty, with new capitals and building projects. This era saw major innovations in irrigation, fortress-building in Nubia, and religious practices. It also laid the groundwork for future periods by developing administrative systems that balanced centralized authority with regional governance. Despite these successes, internal weaknesses and external challenges led eventually to the Second Intermediate Period.

7.2. Reunification Under Mentuhotep II

As we saw in the previous chapter, **Mentuhotep II** (Nebhepetre Mentuhotep) reunited Egypt around **2055 BCE**, bringing an end to the First Intermediate Period. Before his final victory, Upper Egypt had been under Theban leadership, while the Herakleopolitan kings controlled Middle Egypt and the Delta. Mentuhotep II defeated the last Herakleopolitan king, consolidating the north and south under his rule.

7.2.1. Centralizing Authority

Following reunification, Mentuhotep II undertook several measures to ensure control:

- **Administration**: He appointed officials loyal to him, reducing the autonomy of local nomarchs who had grown powerful during the First Intermediate Period.
- **Propaganda**: Temple reliefs and royal inscriptions praised Mentuhotep II as the "Uniter of the Two Lands." This ideological claim reinforced the idea that the king alone guaranteed stability (ma'at) after a chaotic era.
- **Military and Security**: The king likely stationed garrisons in key areas to prevent revolts. He may have launched expeditions into Nubia to secure valuable resources like gold and to keep trade routes safe.

7.2.2. Thebes as a Power Center

Mentuhotep II ruled from **Thebes**, which continued to gain prestige. He constructed a unique funerary complex at **Deir el-Bahari**, blending architecture with the cliff face. This complex served both as his tomb and a site of royal cult worship. The style of this temple influenced later builders, including those in the New Kingdom who also chose Deir el-Bahari for royal monuments.

7.3. Later Eleventh Dynasty Rulers

After Mentuhotep II's long reign, several other kings of the Eleventh Dynasty continued to rule from Thebes:

- **Mentuhotep III** (Sankhkare Mentuhotep): He maintained a reunited Egypt, expanding trade connections. One record mentions an expedition to **Punt** (a region possibly located near the Horn of Africa). This expedition aimed to acquire exotic goods like incense, myrrh, and perhaps wild animals.
- **Mentuhotep IV** (Nebtawyre Mentuhotep): Little is known about him. Some scholars suggest his reign might have ended abruptly or that his successor from a different line usurped the throne.

Over time, political power began to shift northward again, culminating in a new line of rulers known as the **Twelfth Dynasty**, which many consider the golden age of the Middle Kingdom.

7.4. The Rise of the Twelfth Dynasty

Amenemhat I is regarded as the founder of the Twelfth Dynasty (c. 1985 BCE). How he took power is debated—some inscriptions suggest he was a vizier or high official under Mentuhotep IV, then seized the throne. Regardless of the circumstances, Amenemhat I brought stability and introduced reforms that strengthened the monarchy.

7.4.1. Building a New Capital at Itjtawy

One of Amenemhat I's most significant decisions was to establish a new royal residence called **Itjtawy** (also spelled "Ijtawy"), likely located near the Faiyum region, south of Memphis. Although the exact site of Itjtawy is not definitively identified today, it served as the administrative capital:

1. **Strategic Position**: Itjtawy lay in Middle Egypt, convenient for controlling both the south and the north.
2. **Administrative Hub**: Amenemhat I reorganized bureaucracies, placing loyal officials in charge of finances, justice, and regional governance.
3. **Symbolic Fresh Start**: By founding a new capital, the king distanced himself from First Intermediate Period conflicts and signaled a new era of centralized power.

7.4.2. Amenemhat I's Reforms

To limit the influence of powerful nomarchs, Amenemhat I re-established certain Old Kingdom practices:

- **Regular Audits**: Inspectors traveled to nomes, counting livestock, checking irrigation channels, and auditing stored grain.
- **Royal Decrees**: The pharaoh granted land or privileges to temples and officials who demonstrated loyalty, tying them to the crown.
- **Legal Codifications**: Though no single law code from this period survives, administrative texts suggest that Amenemhat I refined legal procedures, making local courts more accountable to the throne.

He also initiated or revived fortress-building projects in Nubia, securing vital trade routes and gold mines.

7.5. Literary Flourish: The "Prophecy of Neferty" and Other Texts

During Amenemhat I's reign, Egyptian literature blossomed. One notable work is the **"Prophecy of Neferty,"** a political text presented as a prophecy from the Old Kingdom. It foretells chaos and disunity, only to be resolved by a savior king named "Ameny." Many scholars interpret this as propaganda meant to legitimize Amenemhat I's rule. It underscores the Middle Kingdom's tendency to look back on the Old Kingdom as a golden age and to position the current king as the restorer of order.

Other literary works from the period include **wisdom texts** (teaching moral and practical lessons) and possibly the earliest forms of stories that blend fiction with moral instructions. This era's increased literacy among some officials and scribes created an environment where such texts could flourish.

7.6. Co-Regency and the Reign of Senusret I

Amenemhat I introduced the practice of **co-regency**, in which the reigning king shared power with his chosen successor for a period. This practice helped ensure smooth transitions and reduce disputes over succession. Amenemhat I selected his son, **Senusret I** (also spelled "Sesostris I"), to rule alongside him before Amenemhat I's death around **1965 BCE**.

7.6.1. Senusret I's Achievements

Senusret I continued to consolidate and expand the Middle Kingdom:

- **Religious Building Projects**: He built and restored temples across Egypt, including shrines at **Heliopolis** for the sun god Re. He also constructed a notable chapel for the god **Min** at **Coptos** in Upper Egypt.
- **Expeditions to Nubia**: Senusret I advanced deeper into Nubia, possibly to the Second Cataract. Fortresses built or enlarged along the Nile ensured control of gold mines and trade routes.
- **Art and Culture**: During Senusret I's reign, art maintained a balance between Old Kingdom traditions and new stylistic choices—sculpture, relief, and jewelry-making flourished.

Like his father, Senusret I also practiced co-regency with his own heir to maintain stable governance.

7.7. The Ongoing Twelfth Dynasty: Amenemhat II, Senusret II, and Senusret III

7.7.1. Amenemhat II (c. 1910–1875 BCE)

Amenemhat II continued many of his predecessors' policies:

- **Trade and Diplomacy**: Egyptian influence abroad grew. Trading expeditions may have reached the Levant, Crete, and Punt. Inscriptions record gifts or tribute from foreign lands.
- **Provincial Monuments**: Several stelae from local governors mention building or restoration projects done "on behalf of Amenemhat II," indicating the king's active oversight of provincial affairs.

7.7.2. Senusret II (c. 1875–1860 BCE)

Senusret II is best known for his focus on **agricultural improvements**:

- **Faiyum Irrigation**: He undertook large-scale drainage and irrigation projects in the **Faiyum** region west of the Nile, creating more arable land. The Faiyum thus became a crucial center for grain production, supporting the kingdom's food supply.
- **Royal Pyramid at Lahun**: Senusret II built his pyramid at **Lahun** (also called "Illahun") near the entrance to the Faiyum. Surrounding it, a planned town housed workers and officials, showing advanced urban planning for the era.

7.7.3. Senusret III (c. 1870–1831 BCE)

Often considered one of the most powerful Middle Kingdom rulers, **Senusret III** undertook military campaigns and restructured the government significantly.

1. **Military Campaigns in Nubia**
   - Expanded Egyptian fortresses near the Second Cataract, including **Semna** and **Kumma**.
   - Created a fortified boundary to control local Nubian chieftains and protect trade routes.
   - Erected boundary stelae proclaiming his victories and establishing Egyptian authority.

2. **Internal Reforms**
     - Senusret III may have reduced the power of the hereditary nomarchs, dividing large provinces or placing them under directly appointed officials.
     - This centralization aimed to prevent any local leader from amassing too much influence, a lesson learned from the First Intermediate Period.
  3. **Royal Imagery**
     - Sculptures of Senusret III often show a more realistic facial expression, including lines and a serious countenance. Some scholars suggest this new portrait style symbolized the king's burden of responsibility or a shift to a more personal representation of kingship.

7.8. Amenemhat III, Amenemhat IV, and Queen Sobekneferu

The later Twelfth Dynasty rulers oversaw a period of prosperity but also faced the kingdom's first signs of strain.

7.8.1. Amenemhat III (c. 1831–1786 BCE)

Amenemhat III is sometimes seen as the last great ruler of the Middle Kingdom. His reign brought:

- **Further Development of the Faiyum**: Building on Senusret II's work, Amenemhat III constructed a colossal water-control system. He also built or expanded a large temple dedicated to **Sobek**, the crocodile god, in the Faiyum region.
- **Massive Construction**: He completed two pyramids—one at **Dahshur** (the "Black Pyramid") and another at **Hawara** near the Faiyum. The Hawara pyramid complex included a labyrinthine mortuary temple described by Greek writers as the "Labyrinth."
- **Intense Resource Exploitation**: Quarry inscriptions show that Amenemhat III expanded mining projects in the Sinai for turquoise and copper, and in the Eastern Desert for gold.

During his long reign, Egypt's economy flourished, though the king's extensive building programs and lavish temple donations may have drained resources over time.

7.8.2. Amenemhat IV and Queen Sobekneferu

Amenemhat IV followed, but his reign appears relatively short. He left fewer records, suggesting a decline in major construction or a possible scarcity of resources. The final monarch of the Twelfth Dynasty was **Queen Sobekneferu**, one of the few female pharaohs in Egypt's history. She reigned only a few years (c. 1806–1802 BCE) and is credited with completing some of Amenemhat III's building projects. Sobekneferu's death ended the Twelfth Dynasty, and her failure to produce an heir may have contributed to political uncertainties that followed.

7.9. Governance and Society in the Middle Kingdom

7.9.1. Royal Power and Bureaucracy

Middle Kingdom rulers learned from the failures of the Old Kingdom's late period and the First Intermediate Period. They worked to balance strong central authority with local governance. To prevent nomarchs from becoming too powerful:

- Some provinces were subdivided to reduce the reach of a single nomarch.
- The throne appointed local officials rather than allowing purely hereditary succession.
- Royal envoys or "overseers" traveled to check on provincial affairs regularly.

7.9.2. Social Classes

1. **King and Royal Family**: At the apex, viewed as divinely chosen protectors of Egypt.
2. **High Officials and Nobles**: Viziers, chancellors, and temple high priests who managed central affairs. Nomarchs or local governors also belonged to this class, though their power was more carefully monitored than before.
3. **Scribes, Craftsmen, and Traders**: A respected class that formed the backbone of Middle Kingdom administration and economy. Scribes controlled documentation, and skilled craftsmen produced goods for temples, tombs, and trade.

4. **Farmers and Laborers**: As in other periods, most Egyptians lived by farming. During flood seasons or major state projects, they could be drafted for labor in construction or maintenance of canals.
5. **Servants and Slaves**: Although not as formally documented as in later societies, there were enslaved or bonded laborers, often prisoners of war or people in debt, who worked on state and private estates.

7.9.3. Daily Life and Culture

Daily life for most Egyptians centered around agriculture, the family household, and local religious traditions. People lived in mudbrick houses, used simple pottery, and relied on the Nile's cycle for planting and harvesting. However, the Middle Kingdom's relative stability and improved irrigation projects meant more consistent harvests for many communities.

Art and Literature blossomed. This era gave us refined jewelry, delicate relief carving, and significant literary works like:

- The **Story of Sinuhe**: A tale of an official who flees Egypt, lives abroad, and returns home later. It offers insights into Egyptian identity and values.
- Didactic texts such as **"The Instruction of King Amenemhat I for His Son Senusret"**, which blends advice on governance with moral lessons.

7.10. Religious Developments in the Middle Kingdom

Religion remained a core part of Egyptian identity:

1. **Amun at Thebes**: The god **Amun** rose in prominence at Thebes, especially as the Theban royals championed him. Over time, Amun merged with Re to become **Amun-Re**, the supreme state deity, although that development continued more fully in the New Kingdom.
2. **Osiris Cult**: Belief in **Osiris**, the god of the afterlife, spread widely. Many Egyptians hoped for an afterlife in the **Field of Reeds**, paralleling Osiris's resurrection.
3. **Funerary Practices**: The "**Coffin Texts**" continued to evolve from earlier Pyramid Texts, making spells and afterlife beliefs more available to non-royal individuals.
4. **Temples and Shrines**: Kings often renovated regional temples, boosting local religious festivals while emphasizing the pharaoh's divine mandate.

7.11. Foreign Relations and Trade

7.11.1. Nubia

Egyptian expansion into **Nubia** was a hallmark of Middle Kingdom policy. Controlling gold mines and trade routes to sub-Saharan Africa was crucial to the economy. Fortresses along the Nile, such as **Buhen**, **Semna**, and **Kumma**, allowed the king to regulate traffic, collect taxes, and deter rebellions. At times, Egyptian armies campaigned deeper south, bringing Nubian leaders under Egyptian influence or installing puppet rulers friendly to Egypt.

7.11.2. The Levant and Beyond

Egypt engaged in trade with **Byblos** (in modern-day Lebanon) for cedar wood and with **Syria-Palestine** for various goods like resin, wine, and metals. Middle Kingdom rulers likely maintained small garrisons or trade outposts in the Sinai Peninsula to protect copper and turquoise mining operations.

There is also limited evidence of contact with the Minoan civilization on **Crete** and possibly other Aegean communities, indicated by finds of Egyptian goods abroad and foreign artifacts within Egyptian port sites.

7.11.3. Punt and the Red Sea

As seen in records from Mentuhotep III's reign, there were voyages to **Punt** for incense, myrrh, and exotic animals. These expeditions demonstrated not only trade but also the pharaoh's ability to project power beyond Egypt's immediate borders.

7.12. Decline of the Middle Kingdom and Transition

Following Sobekneferu's short reign, the **Thirteenth Dynasty** took shape around 1802 BCE. Early on, these kings tried to uphold Middle Kingdom standards, but the royal line became less stable. Records show a rapid turnover of monarchs, with some reigning only a few months or years.

While some Thirteenth Dynasty rulers (like **Sobekhotep II** or **Khendjer**) attempted to maintain centralized power, cracks appeared:

- **Growing Autonomy of Regional Lords**: The old pattern of nomarch influence re-emerged in certain provinces.
- **Economic and Environmental Pressures**: Shifts in the Nile's flood cycles may have caused periodic famines or poor harvests, weakening the state's finances.
- **External Pressures**: New groups began entering the Delta from the east, setting the stage for foreign infiltration in the north.

As the Thirteenth Dynasty progressed, a parallel line called the **Fourteenth Dynasty** may have existed in the eastern Delta, further fracturing royal authority. By around **1650 BCE**, Egypt once again found itself splintered, marking the start of the **Second Intermediate Period**.

7.13. Middle Kingdom Art and Architecture: A Lasting Influence

Despite the later decline, the Middle Kingdom's artistic and architectural legacy influenced subsequent eras. Key features:

1. **Royal Pyramids**: Though smaller than Old Kingdom pyramids, Middle Kingdom pyramids introduced complex interior designs and mortuary temples with labyrinth-like passages.
2. **Temples**: Rulers renovated and expanded older temples, while also building new ones in Thebes, Abydos, Heliopolis, and the Faiyum.
3. **Statues and Reliefs**: Emphasized a mix of idealism (smooth bodies, youthful forms) and realism (detailed facial features in some royal statues).
4. **Jewelry and Craftsmanship**: Goldsmithing and beadwork achieved high levels of refinement, as evidenced by the jewelry sets discovered in royal and noble tombs at sites like **Lahun** and **Dahshur**.

7.14. Lasting Achievements of the Middle Kingdom

1. **Strong Central Government**: Although it eventually weakened, the Middle Kingdom demonstrated a model in which the monarchy carefully balanced local power structures.
2. **Cultural Renaissance**: Literature, art, and religious texts flourished, producing classics like "The Tale of Sinuhe" and refined versions of the Coffin Texts.

3. **Infrastructure**: Expanding farmland in the Faiyum and building fortresses in Nubia showcased Egyptian engineering skills and extended the kingdom's direct influence.
4. **Foreign Trade and Influence**: Diplomatic and commercial ties enriched Egypt, while expansions into Nubia set the stage for more ambitious conquests in the New Kingdom.

7.15. Conclusion of Chapter 7

The Middle Kingdom stands as a time of renewed unity, cultural brilliance, and administrative innovation. Rising from the ashes of the First Intermediate Period, the Eleventh and Twelfth Dynasty pharaohs transformed Thebes into a major political and religious center, then shifted power to a new capital in Middle Egypt. They balanced tradition with new ideas, building on Old Kingdom legacies but avoiding many of its pitfalls.

Yet, success carried seeds of future problems. Heavy spending on building projects, potential changes in the Nile's floods, and the steady infiltration of foreign groups in the north contributed to the eventual fragmentation of the kingdom. As the Thirteenth Dynasty struggled to keep power, Egypt edged toward the **Second Intermediate Period**, a time when foreign rulers—most famously the **Hyksos**—would gain a foothold in the Delta, posing new questions about Egypt's identity and sovereignty.

In the next chapter, we will examine how the kingdom fractured yet again, giving rise to multiple dynasties and allowing outsiders to control parts of the country. We will see how Egyptians in Thebes responded, setting the stage for another dramatic reunification that would usher in the New Kingdom and the age of empire.

CHAPTER 8

THE SECOND INTERMEDIATE PERIOD

8.1. Introduction to the Second Intermediate Period

The **Second Intermediate Period** (c. 1650–1550 BCE) was a time when Egypt was divided once again, this time partly under the control of foreign rulers known as the **Hyksos**. The period extends from the late **Thirteenth Dynasty** through the **Seventeenth Dynasty**, until the **Eighteenth Dynasty** pharaohs reunified the country and founded the New Kingdom.

Key features of the Second Intermediate Period include:

- The breakdown of centralized authority after the Middle Kingdom.
- The rise of the **Hyksos** in the eastern Delta, establishing the **Fifteenth Dynasty**.
- Parallel native Egyptian dynasties in Thebes and possibly other regions.
- Constant political and military struggles, culminating in a Theban victory over the Hyksos.

In this chapter, we will look at how foreign influence reshaped parts of Egypt, how local rulers responded, and how a line of Theban kings eventually regained full control, setting the stage for a new era of strong pharaohs.

8.2. The Late Thirteenth and Fourteenth Dynasties

After the death of **Queen Sobekneferu** (end of the Twelfth Dynasty) around 1802 BCE, the **Thirteenth Dynasty** took power. Early Thirteenth Dynasty kings tried to maintain the Middle Kingdom's administrative system, but they faced growing challenges:

1. **Rapid Succession of Rulers**: Many kings reigned briefly, indicating possible internal conflicts or weak control over succession.
2. **Localized Power**: Nomarchs and local leaders continued to reassert independence.

3. **Foreign Settlers**: Peoples from the Near East—often called **Asiatics**—settled in the eastern Delta, seeking farmland and trade opportunities. Over time, some gained political influence.

Meanwhile, the **Fourteenth Dynasty** may have governed portions of the Delta independently or in parallel with the Thirteenth Dynasty. Evidence is limited, but it suggests further fragmentation of authority in northern Egypt.

8.3. Rise of the Hyksos in the Delta

The term **Hyksos** likely comes from an Egyptian phrase meaning "rulers of foreign lands." By around 1650 BCE, certain foreign elites of Canaanite or Levantine origin had established a stronghold in the eastern Delta, eventually proclaiming themselves kings of Egypt. They formed what we call the **Fifteenth Dynasty**.

8.3.1. Who Were the Hyksos?

Most scholars believe the Hyksos were a mix of Semitic-speaking peoples from the Levant region (modern Syria-Palestine). They gradually migrated into the Delta for economic reasons, trading and intermarrying. When central power weakened, their leaders seized the chance to rule. The Hyksos capital was likely **Avaris** (in the area of modern Tell el-Dab'a).

8.3.2. Hyksos Innovations and Influence

The Hyksos introduced or popularized several technologies in Egypt:

1. **Horse-Drawn Chariot**: Revolutionized warfare and transport.
2. **Composite Bow**: Provided greater range and power.
3. **New Agricultural and Metallurgical Techniques**: Possibly including advanced bronze work.

They adopted many Egyptian customs, titles, and gods. For example, some Hyksos kings used Egyptian royal names and worshiped Egyptian deities like **Seth**, whom they associated with a Semitic storm god.

8.4. The Sixteenth Dynasty and Local Rulers

While the Fifteenth Dynasty Hyksos ruled much of the Delta, other local dynasties emerged in Middle or Upper Egypt. The **Sixteenth Dynasty** is often described as a line of minor kings, possibly ruling Middle Egypt under Hyksos overlordship or acting independently in pockets of territory. Their exact range of control is uncertain due to sparse records.

In many areas, local rulers paid tribute to the Hyksos rather than face conflict. This arrangement allowed some Egyptian nomes to continue everyday life with minimal interference, though they recognized Hyksos sovereignty in official matters.

8.5. Thebes and the Seventeenth Dynasty

Meanwhile, **Thebes** remained an important power center in Upper Egypt. The local rulers there, claiming to be true heirs of the Middle Kingdom, formed the **Seventeenth Dynasty**. Initially, they coexisted with the Hyksos, possibly paying tribute or keeping a neutral stance to avoid direct confrontation.

Over time, Theban rulers grew more assertive:

1. **Reasserting Religious Authority**: They promoted the cult of **Amun**, reinforcing their legitimacy as the rightful guardians of Egyptian tradition.
2. **Building Alliances**: They may have married into influential families or sought support among powerful nomarchs in Upper Egypt.
3. **Preparing for Conflict**: Archaeological evidence suggests Thebans had access to improved weapons, including the horse-drawn chariot, indicating they learned or appropriated Hyksos innovations.

8.6. Key Seventeenth Dynasty Figures

Several Theban kings set the stage for a final showdown with the Hyksos:

- **Intef VII** (Nubkheperre Intef): Continued to strengthen Thebes' position.
- **Sobekemsaf II**: Known from a few stelae and building inscriptions; details are limited, but he helped maintain Theban rule.

- **Seqenenre Tao** (Seqenera Djehuti-aa-en-Re): A pivotal figure who likely began open warfare against the Hyksos. His mummy shows severe head wounds, suggesting he died in battle or was executed after capture.
- **Kamose**: Seqenenre Tao's successor. Kamose launched raids into Middle Egypt, attacking Hyksos strongholds to cut off their supply lines. He left inscriptions boasting about his campaigns.

Kamose described the Hyksos as "Asiatics" who defiled the land, stirring nationalist sentiments among the Theban population. His attacks disrupted Hyksos trade routes, weakening them and setting the stage for the final unification under Kamose's successor.

8.7. Hyksos Rule and Administration

Despite ongoing conflicts, Hyksos rule was not entirely destructive for the Delta region. They established:

1. **Trade Networks**: Maintaining strong ties with the Levant, likely exporting Egyptian grain and importing silver, timber, and other goods.
2. **Cultural Exchange**: Artifacts from Avaris show a blend of Egyptian and Canaanite styles, including pottery and figurines.
3. **Adaptation of Egyptian Bureaucracy**: Hyksos kings used Egyptian scribes, language, and bureaucratic procedures. This continuity helped them govern effectively.

However, the Hyksos never extended full control beyond Lower and parts of Middle Egypt, allowing Thebes and other regions to remain semi-autonomous or even fully independent.

8.8. Warfare and the Struggle for Unification

By the late Seventeenth Dynasty, Theban leaders saw an opportunity to expel the Hyksos completely. The series of conflicts that followed were significant:

- **Military Tactics**: Both sides used chariots, composite bows, and new forms of body armor. Control of strategic fortresses along the Nile was crucial.

- **Diplomacy and Alliances**: Thebes might have formed pacts with Nubian groups, ensuring southern borders stayed secure while focusing on the Hyksos in the north.
- **Naval Movements**: The Nile was a key corridor. Fleets of boats could move troops quickly, while also supporting supply lines.

Kamose's inscriptions from Thebes recount his victories but acknowledge incomplete success—he died before fully driving out the Hyksos. That task fell to his brother (or possibly son), **Ahmose**, who founded the Eighteenth Dynasty.

8.9. End of the Second Intermediate Period: The Reign of Ahmose

Ahmose (Nebpehtyre) led the final campaigns against the Hyksos:

1. **Siege of Avaris**: Egyptian forces besieged the Hyksos capital, ultimately capturing it. Contemporary records mention fierce fighting, destruction of city walls, and many captives.
2. **Pursuit into the Levant**: According to later inscriptions, Ahmose may have followed fleeing Hyksos into southern Palestine, attacking their strongholds there to prevent any regrouping.
3. **Consolidation of Power**: After defeating the Hyksos, Ahmose reestablished a single royal government over all Egypt, from the Delta down to the First Cataract and beyond.

Ahmose's success in reunifying Egypt marks the end of the Second Intermediate Period. He established the **Eighteenth Dynasty**, launching the New Kingdom—an era of expansion, prosperity, and monumental construction.

8.10. Daily Life Under Hyksos and Theban Influence

While much political history focuses on kings and battles, ordinary Egyptians lived day to day in varied ways during the Second Intermediate Period:

- **In the Delta Under Hyksos**: Many farmers continued normal routines, paying taxes in grain or livestock. Some might have encountered new foreign goods or ideas through trade. Craftsmen could produce items for Hyksos elites or for temple complexes that remained active.

- **In Thebes and Upper Egypt**: People observed the growth of the Amun cult, sometimes conscripted into building or military projects. Loyal Theban nomarchs likely had more local power during periods of conflict.
- **Interaction and Mixing**: Egyptians sometimes intermarried with foreigners in the Delta. Language exchange and cultural blending occurred, particularly in border areas or trade towns.

8.11. Artistic and Cultural Developments

The Second Intermediate Period left fewer grand monuments than earlier times, as war and fragmentation limited large-scale state-sponsored projects. Still, there are notable developments:

1. **Regional Styles**: Tombs and artifacts reflect local tastes—some Lower Egyptian tombs show Canaanite-inspired pottery, while Theban tombs continued Middle Kingdom traditions with slight modifications.
2. **Simple Burials**: Many burying practices were modest, reflecting reduced wealth in certain areas. Wood or pottery coffins decorated with incantations (similar to the Coffin Texts) remained common.
3. **Continuity of Religious Beliefs**: Despite foreign rule, Egyptian deities remained central. The Hyksos themselves worshiped some Egyptian gods, blending them with their own. Over time, certain artifacts show the worship of Seth, Baal, and other deities interchangeably.

8.12. Administration and Economy

With two major centers of power (Hyksos in the north, Thebes in the south), administration was highly localized. Each region had its own tax collection, justice system, and scribal bureaucracy. The economy relied on:

- **Agriculture**: As always, the Nile's floods were crucial. In stable areas, farming continued with minimal disruption, but in conflict zones, fields might be abandoned or destroyed.
- **Trade**: The Hyksos connected Egypt more closely with the Levant, encouraging exchange of metal goods, wine, and possibly horses. The Thebans traded with Nubia for gold, cattle, and other resources.
- **Tribute and Warfare**: Armies on both sides seized or taxed local communities. Control of trade routes offered a vital source of revenue.

8.13. Literature and Writing

While no great literary masterpieces from this era rival the Middle Kingdom texts, some documents survive:

- **Administrative Records**: Fragmented papyri detail economic transactions, including shipments of grain, cattle tallies, and fortress rosters.
- **Military Stelae**: Kamose's stela at Karnak is among the best-known texts, boasting of victories against the Hyksos and labeling them as illegitimate rulers.
- **Funerary Texts**: Versions of the Coffin Texts continued, evolving into early forms of what would become the "Book of the Dead" in the New Kingdom.

8.14. The Hyksos Legacy

Although the Hyksos were eventually expelled, they left lasting influences:

1. **Military Technology**: The widespread adoption of the horse-drawn chariot and improved weaponry remained crucial in the upcoming New Kingdom.
2. **Cultural and Artistic Exchange**: Levantine motifs in pottery, metals, and architecture lingered. Over time, Egyptians integrated these ideas into their own styles.
3. **Political Lessons**: The memory of foreign occupation spurred later New Kingdom pharaohs to secure Egypt's northeastern borders vigorously, leading to campaigns in the Levant aimed at creating buffer zones.

8.15. Theban Victory and the Road to the New Kingdom

Ahmose's triumph over the Hyksos laid the foundation for the **Eighteenth Dynasty**, which would become one of the most celebrated dynasties in Egyptian history. After reasserting control over the Delta, Ahmose dealt with rebellious local chieftains and reorganized the administration. He also renewed large building projects, especially in Thebes, dedicating temples to Amun and other gods who were said to have guided him to victory.

In military terms, the momentum continued after Ahmose. His successors, such as **Amenhotep I** and **Thutmose I**, expanded Egypt's borders far into Nubia and the Levant. This transformation of Egypt into a militarily aggressive and territorially vast state marks the early stages of the New Kingdom.

8.16. Comparisons with the First Intermediate Period

Both the **First** and **Second Intermediate Periods** shared certain patterns:

- Decentralized power and rival dynasties.
- The rise of one strong region—Thebes—leading a reunification.
- Cultural diversity and increased local autonomy.

However, the Second Intermediate Period stands out because foreign rule played a key role in the north. This external influence introduced fresh ideas, technologies, and cultural elements that Egyptians absorbed, setting the stage for the New Kingdom's imperial ambitions.

8.17. Daily Realities of Conflict

The frequent warfare between Thebes and the Hyksos impacted many Egyptians, particularly those living in contested borderlands. Some practical consequences might have included:

- **Forced Migration**: Farmers and traders fleeing war zones.
- **Economic Disruption**: Trading routes shifting or closing, leading to shortages or price increases for basic goods.
- **Cultural Exchange**: Refugees, mercenaries, and merchants introduced new music, dialects, and customs as they moved around the region.

Despite hardships, Egyptian culture proved resilient. Many long-standing traditions—writing, burial customs, religious beliefs—continued through the turmoil, albeit with local variations and influences from neighboring cultures.

8.18. Key Sites of the Second Intermediate Period

- **Avaris (Tell el-Dab'a)**: The Hyksos capital in the eastern Delta, featuring mixed Egyptian-Levantine archaeological layers.
- **Thebes (Waset)**: Home base for the Seventeenth Dynasty, site of temples dedicated to Amun.

- **Cusae or other Middle Egypt cities**: Potential shifting front lines between the Hyksos and Thebans.
- **Nubian Fortresses**: Controlled by either Theban rulers or local governors, essential for trade and resources.

8.19. The End of the Second Intermediate Period

By the final years of the Seventeenth Dynasty, Thebes was strong enough to challenge the Hyksos directly. Seqenenre Tao began open hostilities; Kamose continued the attacks, and Ahmose delivered the final blow. The conquest of Avaris and the push into southern Palestine wiped out the Hyksos' base of power, reuniting Egypt.

Historians place the end of the Second Intermediate Period around **1550 BCE**, when Ahmose took the throne of a unified Egypt and inaugurated the Eighteenth Dynasty. With peace in the Delta, the newly united kingdom turned its attention to expansion, architectural innovation, and religious transformation in the centuries to come.

CHAPTER 9

THE NEW KINGDOM

9.1. Introduction to the New Kingdom

The **New Kingdom** spans roughly from **1550 to 1070 BCE**, covering the **Eighteenth, Nineteenth, and Twentieth Dynasties**. Many scholars consider it the most illustrious and expansive phase of ancient Egyptian history. Having expelled the Hyksos at the end of the Second Intermediate Period, the Theban rulers who founded the Eighteenth Dynasty built a powerful, centralized state with the pharaoh at its heart. During the New Kingdom, Egypt became an imperial power, extending its influence into Nubia (to the south) and the Levant (to the northeast).

Monumental architecture, flourishing arts, and complex religious developments characterized this era. Famous names such as **Hatshepsut**, **Thutmose III**, **Amenhotep III**, **Akhenaten**, **Tutankhamun**, **Ramses II**, and **Ramses III** come from this period, each leaving distinct marks on Egypt's political, cultural, and spiritual life. Yet, by the close of the Twentieth Dynasty, internal difficulties and external pressures led to a gradual weakening of centralized authority, setting the stage for the Third Intermediate Period.

9.2. The Eighteenth Dynasty: Reunification and Early Expansion

After defeating the Hyksos, **Ahmose I** (1550–1525 BCE) founded the **Eighteenth Dynasty**, solidifying Theban power over a unified Egypt. He completed the conquest of the Hyksos capital at Avaris and quelled any remaining local resistance in the Delta. He then pushed into southern Palestine to ensure the Hyksos would not return. With the Delta secure, he turned south to Nubia, reaffirming Egyptian dominance over valuable gold mines and trade routes.

9.2.1. Ahmose's Domestic Policies

1. **Restoration of Temples**: Ahmose rebuilt or repaired many temples that had fallen into disrepair, especially in Thebes and Abydos.

2. **Land and Tax Reforms**: The pharaoh rewarded loyal nobles and soldiers with land, stimulating an economy battered by years of conflict.
3. **Administrative Continuity**: Many Middle Kingdom administrative practices continued, but a new generation of officials rose to serve the Theban line. The vizier oversaw taxation, courts, building projects, and foreign policy.

By renewing older traditions and adapting to new realities, Ahmose laid the foundations for a stable and prosperous Eighteenth Dynasty.

9.2.2. Amenhotep I (1525–1504 BCE)

Amenhotep I, Ahmose's son (or close relative), consolidated his father's gains. During his reign:

- **Military Actions**: He may have launched small campaigns in Nubia or along the Sinai, although records are sparse.
- **Religious Building**: He continued focusing on Theban temples, notably at **Karnak**, which evolved into the principal temple complex of Amun-Re.
- **Founding of the Royal Necropolis**: Amenhotep I and his mother, Ahmose-Nefertari, were later revered as patron deities of the **Theban necropolis**. Some traditions link Amenhotep I to the early development of the **Valley of the Kings**, though the earliest clear burials there date a bit later.

When Amenhotep I died, he was succeeded by **Thutmose I**, marking the start of broader territorial ambitions.

9.3. Thutmose I, Thutmose II, and the Emergence of Hatshepsut

9.3.1. Thutmose I (1504–1492 BCE)

Thutmose I married into the royal line—he may have been a military officer or distant royal relative. Under his rule:

1. **Expansion into Nubia**: Thutmose I extended Egyptian authority to the Fourth Cataract of the Nile. Monuments and stelae at sites like **Tombos** record his victories, establishing garrisons and fortifications.

2. **Campaigns in the Levant**: Pharaoh led armies into Syria-Palestine to subdue local chieftains. This laid the groundwork for later expansions by Thutmose III.
3. **Karnak Temple Expansion**: Thutmose I commissioned major additions at Karnak, including obelisks and new courts dedicated to Amun-Re.

9.3.2. Thutmose II (1492–1479 BCE)

Thutmose II succeeded his father, though his reign seems shorter and less documented:

- **Military Control**: Thutmose II dealt with uprisings in Nubia and possibly small revolts in Palestine.
- **Hatshepsut's Influence**: Thutmose II married his half-sister **Hatshepsut**, daughter of Thutmose I by a royal wife. As Great Royal Wife, Hatshepsut gained administrative and religious standing at court.

Thutmose II's early death left the throne to a young heir, **Thutmose III**, while Hatshepsut acted as regent. This situation profoundly shaped Egypt's history in the mid-Eighteenth Dynasty.

9.3.3. The Rise of Hatshepsut (1479–1458 BCE)

Hatshepsut quickly moved from regent to ruling as pharaoh in her own right. She adopted full royal titulary, including wearing male regalia like the false beard and the kingly uraeus.

Key achievements:

1. **Mortuary Temple at Deir el-Bahari**: One of the architectural marvels of ancient Egypt, blending with the cliffs west of Thebes. Scenes within depict her divine birth, legitimizing her reign.
2. **Trade Expedition to Punt**: Her most famous expedition sailed down the Red Sea to Punt (possibly in the Horn of Africa region), returning with myrrh trees, incense, ebony, gold, and exotic animals. This venture boosted the economy and underscored Egypt's maritime capabilities.
3. **Peaceful Policies**: Hatshepsut focused more on diplomacy and trade than on massive military campaigns, though she did maintain earlier conquests in Nubia and the Levant.

Hatshepsut's reign is often viewed as a stable, prosperous period, laying strong foundations for the conquests that Thutmose III would later undertake.

9.4. Thutmose III: The Warrior Pharaoh and Empire Building

Upon Hatshepsut's death, her stepson/nephew **Thutmose III** (1479–1425 BCE) assumed full control. He is widely recognized as one of Egypt's greatest warrior pharaohs.

9.4.1. Early Campaigns in Canaan and Syria

Thutmose III launched multiple campaigns (some sources list up to 17) to subdue rebellious city-states in Canaan and Syria. The most notable was the **Battle of Megiddo** around 1457 BCE:

- **Strategic Surprise**: Instead of taking safer, longer routes, Thutmose III marched his army through a narrow pass, catching the enemy unprepared.
- **Result**: Victory at Megiddo brought many northern Canaanite cities under Egyptian vassalage. Tribute flowed south, and Egyptian administrators kept watch over trade routes.

9.4.2. Further Northern Expansion

Thutmose III campaigned well beyond the Euphrates River, possibly engaging with the kingdom of Mitanni. Although direct conquest of Mitanni was never fully realized in his reign, repeated forays forced local rulers to pay tribute or accept Egyptian overlordship in parts of Syria.

9.4.3. Administration of the Empire

Thutmose III managed newly won territories using a mix of direct governance (Egyptian garrisons and officials) and local vassal kings who pledged loyalty. This structure allowed the pharaoh to tap into vast resources:

- **Gold and Lapis Lazuli**: Flowed from Nubia and the distant east.
- **Timber and Wine**: Came from the Levant.
- **Exotic Goods**: Such as horses, chariots, and metals, enriched the royal treasury.

Thutmose III also built extensively at Karnak, erecting pylons, obelisks, and reliefs celebrating his victories. By the end of his reign, Egypt dominated a large swath of territory from southern Nubia to northern Syria, making it a true empire.

9.5. Amenhotep II, Thutmose IV, and Diplomatic Shifts

9.5.1. Amenhotep II (1427–1400 BCE)

Amenhotep II, Thutmose III's son, continued military campaigns to maintain his father's conquests:

- **Stabilizing Syria-Palestine**: He led raids against rebellious cities. Inscriptions boast of taking many prisoners.
- **Nubian Control**: Amenhotep II's forces quelled any Nubian revolts, ensuring gold mines remained productive.
- **Sporting and Athletic Image**: This king liked to display his prowess in archery and physical challenges, possibly to emphasize martial strength and discourage revolts.

9.5.2. Thutmose IV (1400–1390 BCE)

Thutmose IV is best known for the "**Dream Stela**" at the Great Sphinx in Giza, which claims he became king after being chosen by the Sphinx in a dream. Politically, his reign showed:

- **Diplomacy with Mitanni**: Instead of constant war, Thutmose IV sought alliances. He likely married a Mitannian princess, a move that signaled a shift toward **diplomatic marriages** for peace and prestige.
- **Monument Building**: He repaired the Sphinx and improved temple facilities, though on a smaller scale than Thutmose III.

His relatively brief reign laid the groundwork for a more peaceful approach to foreign relations, culminating under Amenhotep III.

9.6. Amenhotep III: The Zenith of the Eighteenth Dynasty

Amenhotep III (1390–1352 BCE) presided over one of the most stable and prosperous periods in Egyptian history. He inherited an empire at its peak.

9.6.1. Peace and Diplomacy

Amenhotep III favored **diplomacy** over large-scale military campaigns. He maintained borders through:

1. **Royal Marriages**: Took foreign princesses from Babylon, Mitanni, and Arzawa, forging alliances.
2. **Tribute and Gift Exchange**: Letters found at **Amarna** (though from later times) hint that Amenhotep III and his son Amenhotep IV (Akhenaten) corresponded with other Near Eastern rulers, exchanging lavish gifts to maintain goodwill.

9.6.2. Monumental Construction

- **Luxor Temple**: Amenhotep III built much of the core structure dedicated to Amun.
- **Karnak Expansions**: He added a massive third pylon and many statues.
- **Mortuary Temple** in Western Thebes: Now mostly destroyed, except for the famous **Colossi of Memnon**, two giant seated statues that once guarded the temple's entrance.
- **Malkata Palace**: A huge royal palace complex near Thebes, featuring a lake for leisure boat rides.

His building program showcased the wealth and confidence of the Eighteenth Dynasty. The use of skilled artisans, elaborate reliefs, and massive stone elements emphasized a golden age.

9.6.3. Religious and Cultural Developments

Amenhotep III highlighted his divine association, calling himself the "Dazzling Sun Disc." Although the full solar-oriented cult worship would peak under his successor, Amenhotep III's own emphasis on the solar aspects of Amun-Re foreshadowed changes. Meanwhile, art under his rule displayed elegance and realism, evident in statues, jewelry, and palace decorations.

9.7. Akhenaten and the Religious Revolution

Amenhotep III's successor, **Amenhotep IV**, changed his name to **Akhenaten** (1352–1336 BCE) and introduced one of the most radical shifts in Egyptian religion and art.

9.7.1. The Aten Cult

Akhenaten championed the worship of **Aten**, the sun disc, above all other gods. He proclaimed Aten as the sole creator and life force, effectively sidelining the dominant Amun priesthood in Thebes. Key actions:

1. **Founding a New Capital**: Akhenaten built **Akhetaten** (modern **Amarna**) in Middle Egypt. He moved the court there, breaking with Theban traditions.
2. **Closing or Reducing Other Temples**: Inscriptions record diminished funding for Amun temples, though how severely they were closed remains debated.
3. **Artistic Changes**: "Amarna art" depicted the royal family with elongated limbs and heads, intimate family scenes, and a focus on sunlight as a divine force.

9.7.2. Impact on Foreign Policy and Administration

While Akhenaten devoted himself to religious transformation, Egyptian vassals in Syria-Palestine faced increasing threats from rival powers like the Hittites. The **Amarna Letters**—a cache of diplomatic correspondence—show local rulers pleading for Egyptian intervention, often with minimal response. The empire may have weakened at its margins during his reign.

9.7.3. Nefertiti's Role

Queen Nefertiti played a prominent part, appearing alongside Akhenaten in major ceremonies and official art. Some sources suggest she may have served as co-regent, though details remain speculative. Regardless, she was central to the new religious ideology, sharing the divine worship of Aten with her husband.

9.8. Restoration under Tutankhamun, Ay, and Horemheb

Akhenaten's religious experiment did not last long. After his death, a series of rulers reversed his policies.

9.8.1. Tutankhaten / Tutankhamun (1336–1327 BCE)

Initially named **Tutankhaten**, the young king changed his name to **Tutankhamun**, signifying a return to the worship of Amun. Under influential advisers (possibly including the court official **Ay** and the general **Horemheb**), Tutankhamun:

- **Reopened Amun Temples**: Restored funds and priests to the old cults.
- **Left Amarna**: The royal court moved back to Memphis and Thebes, abandoning Akhetaten.
- **Limited Military Action**: The empire still struggled, but Tutankhamun's short reign saw attempts to regain stability.

He died around age 19, leaving no direct heir. His tomb in the Valley of the Kings, discovered nearly intact in modern times, revealed the opulence of even a relatively minor pharaoh.

9.8.2. Ay (1327–1323 BCE)

Ay, likely an older court official and possibly a relative of Nefertiti, succeeded Tutankhamun. His brief reign continued the restoration of traditional religion but left little lasting impact. Some scholars believe he married Tutankhamun's widow, Ankhesenamun, to legitimize his throne.

9.8.3. Horemheb (1323–1295 BCE)

A powerful general, **Horemheb** seized power after Ay's death. He finished dismantling the Atenist reforms:

- **Temple Restorations**: Horemheb resumed large building campaigns, reusing stones from Akhenaten's monuments for new structures.
- **Legal and Administrative Reforms**: He issued decrees to curb corruption and reorganize the bureaucracy.
- **Succession**: Having no son, Horemheb likely appointed his own successor, **Paramessu**, who became Ramses I. This transition concluded the Eighteenth Dynasty and opened the Nineteenth.

9.9. The Nineteenth Dynasty: Seti I and Ramses II

9.9.1. Ramses I and the Short Reign

Ramses I (1295–1294 BCE) was a seasoned military officer under Horemheb. His brief reign set the foundation for his successors, **Seti I** and **Ramses II**, to restore Egyptian might.

9.9.2. Seti I (1294–1279 BCE)

Seti I aimed to reconquer lost territories:

1. **Campaigns in the Levant**: He fought the Hittites for control of northern Syria, regaining many posts but facing stiff opposition.
2. **Monumental Building**: Seti I constructed a magnificent temple at **Abydos** dedicated to Osiris and other gods, famous for its high-quality reliefs. He also continued expansions at Karnak.
3. **Focus on Traditional Religion**: By rededicating major temples, Seti I reinforced the role of the pharaoh as a pious restorer of ma'at after the disruptions of the Amarna Period.

Though successful militarily, Seti I's gains remained contested, especially by the Hittites. His son, Ramses II, inherited the task of stabilizing Egypt's northern frontier.

9.10. Ramses II: The Great Builder and Diplomacy

Ramses II (1279–1213 BCE), often called "Ramses the Great," ruled for about 66 years. He is famous for his extensive building projects, long reign, and the **Battle of Kadesh** against the Hittites.

9.10.1. The Battle of Kadesh (c. 1274 BCE)

- **Hittite Rivalry**: The city of **Kadesh**, near the Orontes River (in modern Syria), was strategic for controlling trade and influence in the region.
- **Grand Scale**: Both the Egyptians and the Hittites fielded large chariot armies. Ramses II nearly suffered defeat due to Hittite ambush tactics. However, Egyptian reliefs celebrate Ramses's personal bravery, claiming a sort of stalemate or symbolic victory.
- **Outcome**: Kadesh remained under Hittite influence, but Ramses II maintained enough pressure to lead, years later, to the world's earliest known **peace treaty** with the Hittite king, Hattusili III. This treaty stabilized the northern frontier for the remainder of Ramses's reign.

9.10.2. Monumental Construction

Ramses II's building projects outshone even those of previous pharaohs:

1. **Ramesseum**: His mortuary temple at Thebes, featuring colossal statues and grand pylons.
2. **Abu Simbel**: Two massive rock-cut temples in Nubia. The larger temple's facade has four colossal seated figures of Ramses II, demonstrating his power and his deification alongside the gods.
3. **Additions to Karnak and Luxor**: He erected colossal statues and reliefs boasting of military feats.
4. **Pi-Ramesses**: A new capital in the eastern Delta, possibly near the old Hyksos city of Avaris, reflecting a strategic location closer to the Levant.

9.10.3. Diplomatic Marriage and Peace

Ramses II married a Hittite princess after signing the peace treaty, cementing an alliance between the two powers. This approach mirrored earlier practices of international diplomacy through royal marriages.

Ramses II's reign brought relative prosperity, though the cost of colossal building, prolonged warfare, and a large royal family (he had many wives and over 100 children) strained resources.

9.11. Later Nineteenth and Twentieth Dynasties: From Merenptah to Ramses III

9.11.1. Merenptah (1213–1203 BCE)

Merenptah, Ramses II's thirteenth son, inherited the throne at an advanced age. He faced invasions from **Libyans** and "Sea Peoples" on Egypt's western frontier. The **Merenptah Stele** mentions a victory over forces in Canaan, including a reference to a group called "Israel."

Though Merenptah succeeded in defending Egypt, these attacks foreshadowed greater unrest to come.

9.11.2. Twentieth Dynasty and Ramses III (1186–1155 BCE)

After a few short reigns, **Ramses III** rose to power, often viewed as the last great pharaoh of the New Kingdom. Key points:

1. **Defeating the Sea Peoples**: Ramses III claimed victories over these maritime raiders who devastated many Eastern Mediterranean cultures

around 1200 BCE. Battles near the Nile Delta ended in Egyptian success, ensuring Egypt survived while other states collapsed.
2. **Economic Pressures**: Large building projects—like Ramses III's mortuary temple at **Medinet Habu**—and constant warfare drained the treasury. Grain shortages and inflation led to labor strikes, including a famous workers' strike at **Deir el-Medina**.
3. **Internal Conspiracies**: Toward the end of Ramses III's reign, the so-called "Harem Conspiracy" aimed to assassinate him. Though possibly foiled, it indicated mounting unrest at court.

Ramses III's successors (Ramses IV, V, VI, VII, VIII, IX, X, XI) struggled to maintain the empire. Nubia gradually drifted away from direct control, and Egyptian authority in Canaan and Syria diminished.

9.12. Cultural, Religious, and Social Life in the New Kingdom

9.12.1. Flourishing Arts

- **Temple Reliefs**: Scenes of pharaohs offering to gods or smiting enemies. Detailed, vibrant polychrome painting.
- **Sculpture**: From colossal stone statues (Ramses II at Abu Simbel) to smaller, lifelike representations of nobles and officials.
- **Tomb Painting and Book of the Dead**: Nobles' tombs displayed lively images of daily life and funerary rituals. The "**Book of the Dead**" gained popularity, listing spells to help the deceased navigate the afterlife.

9.12.2. Religious Traditions

- **Dominance of Amun**: The cult of Amun at Karnak and Luxor grew wealthy through royal endowments and tribute from conquered lands.
- **Royal Deification**: Pharaohs often presented themselves in divine roles, especially in temples, blending with the worship of major gods such as Amun, Ra, Ptah, and Osiris.
- **Funerary Customs**: Royalty were buried in the **Valley of the Kings** and **Valley of the Queens**, using lavish goods and elaborate tomb decorations. Nobles were buried in private tombs around Thebes and other necropoleis.

9.12.3. Society and Economy

- **Empire Wealth**: Tribute from Nubia and the Levant funded monumental projects. Slaves or prisoners of war sometimes worked on state estates, though the details of their status vary.
- **Rise of Military Elite**: Successful generals could become influential statesmen or even pharaohs (as with Horemheb).
- **Trade Networks**: Reached into the Aegean (Crete, Mycenae), Cyprus, Punt, and beyond. Luxuries like cedar, wine, ivory, and spices flowed into Egypt's markets.

9.13. The Decline of the New Kingdom

By the reign of **Ramses XI** (c. 1107–1070 BCE), centralized power had eroded. Many factors contributed:

1. **Economic Strain**: Heavy military spending, lavish building, and reduced tribute from lost territories caused shortages.
2. **Libyan Pressure**: Tribes migrating into the Delta grew influential, some mercenaries even serving in the Egyptian army.
3. **Priestly Power**: The **High Priests of Amun** at Thebes controlled large estates and nearly formed a state within a state.
4. **Local Fragmentation**: The viceroys of Nubia, local governors, and priesthoods acted semi-independently.

Ramses XI's reign ended with the country effectively split between Lower Egypt (controlled by a dynastic line based at Tanis) and Upper Egypt (dominated by the High Priest of Amun at Thebes). This division marks the dawn of the **Third Intermediate Period**.

CHAPTER 10

THE THIRD INTERMEDIATE PERIOD

10.1. Introduction to the Third Intermediate Period

The **Third Intermediate Period** spans roughly from **1070 to 664 BCE**, covering the **Twenty-First through the Twenty-Fifth Dynasties**. This era began after the collapse of the New Kingdom, when Egypt lost much of its imperial territory and faced internal divisions. Power fractured among various groups:

- **Kings in Tanis (Lower Egypt)**
- **High Priests of Amun in Thebes (Upper Egypt)**
- Later, **Libyan** chieftains who formed new ruling lines
- Eventually, **Kushite (Nubian)** kings who conquered Egypt from the south

Although later Egyptians sometimes viewed this period as chaotic, it included moments of stability and cultural revival. Temples remained important centers of local identity, and certain dynasties, such as the Twenty-Fifth ("Kushite") Dynasty, tried to restore older traditions. Ultimately, the Third Intermediate Period ended with the **Assyrian invasions** in the mid-seventh century BCE and the rise of the **Saite kings** in the Twenty-Sixth Dynasty, leading into the Late Period.

10.2. The Twenty-First Dynasty: Tanis and Theban Divisions

Shortly before the death of **Ramses XI** (end of the New Kingdom), a general named **Smendes** (Nesbanebdjed) established his power in the Delta city of **Tanis**, founding the **Twenty-First Dynasty** (c. 1070–945 BCE). Meanwhile, the High Priest of Amun at Thebes controlled Upper Egypt.

10.2.1. Tanis as the Northern Capital

Smendes and his successors, such as **Amenemope** and **Psusennes I**, ruled the north from Tanis:

- **Royal Tombs** at Tanis: Some Twenty-First Dynasty kings built modest royal tombs here. The tomb of **Psusennes I** famously contained rich grave goods, including a stunning solid silver coffin.
- **Diplomacy and Limited Power**: Without the resources of a fully united empire, these kings managed local issues and sought to maintain peaceful relations with Thebes.

10.2.2. The High Priesthood of Amun in Thebes

Simultaneously, the **High Priests of Amun** held authority in the south:

- **Hereditary Priesthood**: Positions often passed from father to son, intertwining religious and political power.
- **Nominal Loyalty to Tanis**: The Theban clergy acknowledged the kings at Tanis in name, but governed Upper Egypt quite independently.
- **Economic Base**: Control of large temple estates, farmland, and donations from pious elites allowed them to govern effectively.

Though Egypt was not officially divided into separate kingdoms, in practice, the north and south operated under different leadership. Often, family connections—through intermarriages—helped keep some semblance of unity.

10.3. The Twenty-Second Dynasty (Libyan Pharaohs)

Around **945 BCE**, **Shoshenq I** (also spelled Sheshonq) seized power, establishing the **Twenty-Second Dynasty**. Shoshenq I was of **Libyan** descent, part of a group known as the **Meshwesh** or **Ma**, who had settled in the Delta for generations, sometimes serving as mercenaries in the Egyptian army.

10.3.1. Shoshenq I (945–924 BCE)

- **Consolidating Egypt**: Shoshenq I aimed to unify the country. He placed relatives in key priestly positions, including the role of High Priest of Amun, bridging the north-south divide.
- **Military Campaigns**: Some inscriptions suggest he led campaigns into the Levant, possibly to reassert Egyptian influence. Later biblical sources (though from another culture's perspective) associate "Shishak" with an invasion of Judah, though details remain debated.
- **Building Work**: At Karnak, Shoshenq I erected monuments to legitimize his reign. He also reused blocks from earlier structures, continuing a

long-standing Egyptian practice when resources were scarce or to signal continuity.

10.3.2. Later Libyan Rulers

Shoshenq I's descendants ruled for about a century, but power gradually dispersed. Key figures include:

- **Osorkon I**: Maintained high-level building projects but faced internal competition.
- **Takelot I, Osorkon II, Shoshenq III**: With each reign, local branches of the royal family or other Libyan warlords gained autonomy, sometimes founding overlapping dynasties.
- **Control of Thebes**: While some Libyan pharaohs installed family members as High Priests of Amun, Thebes often had its own separate line of priests, creating multiple spheres of authority.

This fragmentation became more pronounced over time, leading to the creation of parallel dynasties in different regions.

10.4. The Twenty-Third and Twenty-Fourth Dynasties: Further Fragmentation

As the Twenty-Second Dynasty weakened, local leaders claimed kingship in various areas, generating the **Twenty-Third Dynasty** (often ruling from Thebes or other southern cities) and the short-lived **Twenty-Fourth Dynasty** (centered around **Sais** in the western Delta).

10.4.1. The Twenty-Third Dynasty

Often overlapping in time with the late Twenty-Second Dynasty:

- **Petubastis I, Osorkon III, Takelot III, Rudamun**: These rulers occasionally recognized or fought each other. The lineages can be confusing due to incomplete records, but overall they show further disunity.
- **Thebes as a Power Center**: Some Twenty-Third Dynasty kings, like **Osorkon III**, succeeded in controlling Thebes, even bridging north-south divides for short periods. Temples remained focal points of local support.

10.4.2. The Twenty-Fourth Dynasty at Sais

Tefnakht and later **Bakenranef** (Bocchoris, per Greek sources) formed the brief Twenty-Fourth Dynasty in the Delta city of **Sais**. They tried to claim authority over Lower Egypt, challenging the Libyan rulers in other Delta regions. However, they soon encountered a far greater force from the south: the Kushites of Nubia, who would establish the Twenty-Fifth Dynasty.

10.5. The Rise of the Kushite (Nubian) Twenty-Fifth Dynasty

Nubia (Kush), south of the First Cataract, had been under Egyptian influence since the Middle and New Kingdoms. As the New Kingdom declined, Kushite rulers became more independent, eventually forming a strong state centered around **Napata**.

10.5.1. Kashta and Piye (Piankhi)

- **Kashta**: A Nubian king who expanded his control northward, possibly influencing Thebes. He recognized the significance of the Amun cult to bolster his legitimacy.
- **Piye (c. 744–714 BCE)**: Kashta's successor, Piye launched a major campaign into Egypt. His triumph is recorded on the "**Victory Stela**," describing how he overcame local rulers in the Delta, including Tefnakht of Sais. Piye insisted on religious submission, commanding each conquered region to worship Amun.

By the time Piye finished, he had established **Kushite rule** over much of Egypt, uniting the country under the Twenty-Fifth Dynasty. Piye then returned to Nubia, preferring to govern from the south but leaving representatives to manage Delta affairs.

10.5.2. Shabaka, Shebitku, and Taharqa

Following Piye, other Nubian pharaohs fully embraced the role of Egyptian kings:

- **Shabaka** (c. 712–698 BCE): Tried to restore old traditions, refurbishing temples, and adopting classical Middle Kingdom and Old Kingdom styles in art.
- **Shebitku** (c. 698–690 BCE): Continued these policies, but faced pressure from expanding powers in the Near East.

- **Taharqa** (c. 690–664 BCE): Reached the peak of Nubian influence. He built extensively at Karnak and elsewhere, championing a revival of Egyptian religious traditions. At the same time, **Assyrian** expansion posed a serious threat from the northeast.

10.6. Religious and Cultural Aspects of the Third Intermediate Period

Despite political fragmentation, religious and cultural life continued to evolve:

1. **Temple-Centered Communities**: Local temples served as social, economic, and religious hubs. They provided jobs, stored surplus grain, and offered a sense of identity amid political chaos.
2. **Artistic Styles**: Many rulers in the Third Intermediate Period looked back to earlier epochs for inspiration. Kushite pharaohs in particular revived Old Kingdom and Middle Kingdom imagery to legitimize their reign.
3. **Burial Practices**: While grand royal tombs like those of the New Kingdom were no longer typical in Thebes, local officials and lesser kings still built tombs in places such as Tanis, Thebes, and Napata (in Nubia). The concept of an afterlife remained deeply ingrained, so coffin styles, shabti figurines, and amulets continued to develop regionally.

10.7. Political Dynamics and Foreign Relations

10.7.1. Libyan Influence

Large numbers of Libyans had settled in the Delta since the late New Kingdom, forming a major segment of the population. Libyan chieftains rose to power, either cooperating with or challenging the nominal pharaoh. Some took on Egyptian titles and married into local noble families. Over time, certain Libyan groups, like the Bubastite line, blended Egyptian and Libyan customs.

10.7.2. Near Eastern Pressures

The major threat to Egyptian autonomy came from Mesopotamia, where the **Assyrian** empire expanded westward. Rival city-states and smaller Levantine powers also impacted trade routes. With the empire lost in the north, Egyptian dynasties had to work hard to protect the Delta.

10.7.3. Nubian Rule and the Confrontation with Assyria

When the Nubian pharaohs of the Twenty-Fifth Dynasty controlled Lower Egypt, they inevitably clashed with Assyrian ambitions. By **671 BCE**, King **Esarhaddon** of Assyria invaded Egypt, capturing Memphis. **Taharqa** retreated to Upper Egypt. Though Taharqa tried to mount counterattacks, repeated invasions led by Esarhaddon's successor, **Ashurbanipal**, forced the Nubians to abandon the Delta completely by **c. 663 BCE**.

In the following power vacuum, local Egyptian leaders in the Delta, especially in Sais, rose to prominence—leading into the **Late Period** with the Saite line of kings (Twenty-Sixth Dynasty).

10.8. The Role of Thebes and the High Priests of Amun

Throughout the Third Intermediate Period, Thebes and its Amun priesthood remained crucial:

1. **Economic Power**: Vast temple lands funded large priestly communities.
2. **Priestly Dynasties**: Some high priests effectively became pharaohs in all but name, minting their own authority with religious backing.
3. **Shifting Loyalties**: At times, Theban priests accepted the Tanite or Libyan kings; at other times, they aligned with Nubian rulers who strongly supported Amun's cult.
4. **Decline of Theban Influence**: As foreign invasions increased and power centers shifted to the Delta, Thebes sometimes faced economic decline or lost direct control over southern territories.

10.9. Daily Life and Society in the Third Intermediate Period

Political fragmentation had mixed impacts on ordinary Egyptians:

- **Local Autonomy**: Many regions managed their own affairs under local lords or priests. This sometimes allowed for quick adaptation to crises, as local leaders responded to the needs of farmers and tradespeople.
- **Economic Instability**: Warfare, shifting rulers, and tribute demands could disrupt trade and agriculture. Some taxes might have been paid multiple times if rival dynasts claimed the same territory.

- **Cultural Blending**: Libyans and Nubians in positions of power introduced some of their customs. Over generations, these cultural elements merged with established Egyptian traditions, creating a diverse but still cohesive identity.
- **Religious Continuity**: The average person continued worshiping local gods, offering small personal donations, and hoping for a secure afterlife. Craftsmen still produced funerary items, though the scale was modest compared to the grand tombs of the New Kingdom elites.

10.10. Artistic Developments and Innovations

During the Third Intermediate Period, art retained many classical Egyptian traits but also showcased regional adaptations:

1. **Tanite Silver Coffins**: Kings like Psusennes I used precious metals for coffins, possibly signifying both status and the availability of silver from trade networks.
2. **Nubian Artistic Influence**: Kushite rulers adopted Egyptian forms (like the double uraeus on their crowns) but added unique Nubian elements, such as distinctive head-shapes in sculpture or local clothing styles.
3. **Temple Restorations**: Despite limited resources, some dynasts restored sections of Karnak or other temples to legitimize their rule by linking it to revered pharaohs of the past.

10.11. The Final Phase: Transition to the Late Period

By **664 BCE**, after repeated Assyrian interventions, Nubian power in Egypt ended. A local Saite prince, **Psamtik I**, emerged as the victor, effectively founding the **Twenty-Sixth Dynasty** and the onset of what historians label the **Late Period**. This moment marks the conclusion of the Third Intermediate Period. In summary:

- **Kushite Retreat**: The last Kushite pharaoh, **Tantamani**, left Memphis and retreated to Nubia.
- **Saite Ascendancy**: Psamtik I reunified Egypt, restoring stability from the Delta city of Sais.
- **New Foreign Influences**: Contacts with Greek mercenaries and traders expanded, though full "modern" interactions are still beyond our scope.

The Third Intermediate Period thus ended with another unification, but Egypt's days of complete independence were numbered, as future threats from the Neo-Babylonians, Persians, and eventually Alexander the Great awaited in the Late Period and beyond.

10.12. Legacy of the Third Intermediate Period

Though often overshadowed by the grandeur of the New Kingdom and the later conquests of the Late Period, the Third Intermediate Period was an important chapter:

1. **Cultural Adaptation**: Egyptians showed resilience, preserving core beliefs in the face of Libyan and Nubian rulership.
2. **Religious Vitality**: Temples kept thriving locally, and the cult of Amun remained an anchor for national unity, even if political unity was lacking.
3. **Shifting Power Centers**: Cities like Tanis, Bubastis, Sais, and Napata rose to prominence, reflecting the period's fluidity.
4. **Prelude to Further Change**: The period laid the groundwork for the Late Period, during which new waves of foreign influence and military challenges shaped Egyptian civilization.

Despite divisions and foreign leadership, ancient Egypt continued to show remarkable continuity in language, religious traditions, and social structures. The complex tapestry of local rulers, high priests, and foreign dynasties demonstrates both the fragility and the adaptability of Egyptian society after the fall of the New Kingdom.

CHAPTER 11

THE LATE PERIOD

11.1. Introduction to the Late Period (664–332 BCE)

The **Late Period** in Egyptian history is generally dated from **664 BCE**, when a new line of native rulers emerged from the city of **Sais** in the western Delta (the Saite Dynasty, or Dynasty 26), until **332 BCE**, when **Alexander the Great** conquered Egypt. This era follows the Third Intermediate Period, a phase marked by political fragmentation and the rise of foreign dynasties (Libyan and Kushite) alongside local rulers.

During the Late Period, Egypt experienced both a **cultural revival** and continued threats from powerful empires such as **Assyria**, **Babylonia**, and eventually **Persia**. The Saite kings attempted to restore a sense of unity and tradition, drawing on older artistic styles and religious customs. They also encouraged trade and diplomatic ties with the Greek world, leading to an influx of **Greek mercenaries** and merchants in the Delta. Despite these successes, the country would face a major turning point when **Persian forces** invaded in **525 BCE**. In this chapter, we focus on the years leading up to that conquest, ending just before the Persian takeover.

11.2. The Rise of the Saite Dynasty (Twenty-Sixth Dynasty)

11.2.1. Psamtik I (664–610 BCE) and the Reunification of Egypt

Egypt emerged from the Third Intermediate Period in a fragmented condition. The **Nubian (Kushite) Twenty-Fifth Dynasty** held Thebes and parts of Upper Egypt until repeated **Assyrian invasions** weakened their power. Local Delta rulers then asserted control. Among them was **Psamtik I** (also spelled Psammetichus), who rose to prominence in **Sais**.

1. **Eliminating Rivals**: Psamtik I capitalized on the departure of the Nubian kings, forging alliances with powerful Delta cities. He eventually asserted his authority over Memphis and Upper Egypt, effectively reuniting the country under Saite rule.

2. **Foreign Alliances**: He maintained a cautious relationship with the Assyrians who had helped him eliminate Nubian control, but he also sought independence once his power was secure.
3. **Greek Mercenaries**: Psamtik I invited Greek warriors—often referred to as "**Ionian**" or "Carian" mercenaries—to bolster his army. Stationed primarily in the Delta, these mercenaries introduced new military practices and fostered cross-cultural exchange.

By the time Psamtik I fully consolidated the kingdom, he had ushered in a new sense of unity and stability not seen since the decline of the New Kingdom.

11.2.2. Saite Administration and Reforms

Under Psamtik I and his successors, the Saite administration sought to:

- **Centralize Power**: Local governors (nomarchs) had held significant autonomy in earlier centuries. The Saite pharaohs reasserted royal authority, placing trusted officials—often with ties to the Delta—throughout the country.
- **Military Modernization**: Alongside traditional Egyptian troops, the pharaohs maintained Greek and other foreign mercenaries. These forces served as an effective standing army, securing borders against threats from Nubia, Libya, or potential eastern invaders.
- **Cultural Revival**: Artists, architects, and scribes drew inspiration from Old Kingdom and Middle Kingdom models. Statues, temple reliefs, and royal iconography often imitated the forms of much earlier dynasties, lending Saite rule an air of legitimacy and nostalgia.

11.2.3. Psamtik I's Successors: Necho I, Psamtik II, and Apries

Though Psamtik I himself reigned until **610 BCE**, other important Saite kings helped shape the later part of the dynasty:

- **Necho I (likely reigned briefly, c. 672–664 BCE)**: He was Psamtik I's father or close predecessor, also based in Sais. His role in founding the Twenty-Sixth Dynasty remains partly unclear due to conflicting evidence, but he set the stage for Psamtik's rise.
- **Psamtik II (595–589 BCE)**: Led a campaign into Nubia, reaching as far south as the Third Cataract. He recorded inscriptions at Abu Simbel,

showing a continued Egyptian interest in securing gold mines and trade routes.
- **Apries (Wahibre, 589–570 BCE)**: Entered into alliances with states in the Levant. He attempted to intervene in the region when Babylon threatened smaller kingdoms, reflecting Egypt's desire to keep a buffer zone in Palestine. However, Apries faced internal dissent, partly due to military failures abroad.

These rulers preserved Saite hegemony, but tensions with Babylon and local crises began to strain the kingdom's resources.

11.3. Foreign Policy and Conflicts During the Saite Era

11.3.1. Relations with the Neo-Assyrian Empire

Initially, Psamtik I owed some debt to the Assyrians, who had weakened the Kushite hold on Egypt. Yet, as Assyria declined in the late 7th century BCE under pressure from the **Neo-Babylonian Empire**, Psamtik and his successors carefully distanced themselves. Egypt maintained sporadic conflict with or support to Levantine states, depending on shifting power balances.

11.3.2. Encounters with Babylonia

By the time of **Necho II** (610–595 BCE), Babylonia emerged as the leading force in Mesopotamia. Necho II attempted to counter Babylonian advances in the Near East:

- **Battle of Carchemish (c. 605 BCE)**: Egyptian forces joined with the remnants of Assyria against the Babylonians, led by **Nebuchadnezzar II**. The Babylonians emerged victorious, consolidating their hold on Syria-Palestine.
- **Egyptian Naval and Canal Projects**: Necho II explored creating a canal linking the Nile to the Red Sea. Though incomplete, the project showcased Egyptian ambition to facilitate trade with the Red Sea and beyond.

Despite Egyptian efforts, Babylonia dominated the region, curbing Egypt's expansion. However, Babylonia did not fully invade Egypt. Instead, a tense standoff and occasional skirmishes characterized their relationship.

11.3.3. Libyan and Nubian Borders

Saite rulers carefully guarded Egypt's western and southern frontiers:

- **Western Border (Libya)**: Various Libyan tribal groups moved near or into the Delta. While the New Kingdom had once integrated some Libyans into Egyptian society, the Saite period saw new waves of potential raids. Fortified outposts and local garrisons mitigated the threat.
- **Nubia**: Nubian states south of Elephantine sometimes challenged or negotiated with Egypt for control of trade routes. Psamtik II's campaign indicated ongoing Egyptian interest in reasserting dominance there, though it was never as extensive as New Kingdom rule had been.

11.4. Internal Developments and Cultural Renaissance

Despite foreign pressures, the Saite period is often seen as a time of **cultural renaissance** within Egypt.

11.4.1. Architectural Projects

Saite pharaohs rebuilt or renovated many temples, particularly in the Delta and around Memphis:

1. **Sais**: The hometown of the Saite dynasty contained temples to Neith and other deities. Although few ruins survive, ancient sources mention impressive structures.
2. **Memphis**: Ongoing worship of Ptah led to expansions and repairs. Memphis also served as a cultural crossroads, hosting Greek merchants and artisans.
3. **Karnak and Other Sites**: Some building work in Thebes continued, though on a smaller scale than in earlier eras, partly because the Delta became the new power center.

11.4.2. Literature and Learning

- **Historical Texts**: Scribes compiled king lists and genealogies, celebrating the unity restored under Saite rulers.
- **Religious Writings**: Hymns to deities like Neith, Ptah, and Amun reflect continuing devotion. The Book of the Dead was copied and elaborated with Saite stylistic flourishes.

- **Science and Medicine**: Greek visitors wrote accounts of Egyptian medical knowledge, mathematics, and architecture. The Greek historian **Herodotus** later traveled in Egypt (though somewhat after the Saite heyday), describing its customs with both curiosity and inaccuracies.

11.4.3. Art and Sculpture

Saite art blended **archaizing** elements—imitating Old Kingdom and Middle Kingdom forms—with contemporary refinements:

- **Statues**: Pharaohs and officials wore styles of dress reminiscent of older periods. Facial features could be more realistic, hinting at personal identity beneath the timeless style.
- **Reliefs**: Temple reliefs used delicate lines and sharp detailing, sometimes on smaller stone blocks.
- **Metalwork**: Bronze statuettes of deities (like the cat goddess Bastet or the ibis-headed Thoth) became more common, partly for the votive market.

This cultural revival and pride in ancient heritage helped the Saite kings legitimize their reign and foster a sense of national identity.

11.5. The Reign of Amasis (Ahmose II, 570–526 BCE)

One of the most notable Saite pharaohs was **Amasis** (also spelled Ahmose II). He came to power after a rebellion deposed Apries, the previous ruler.

1. **Consolidation of Power**: Amasis initially faced internal strife because many elites remained loyal to Apries. By offering amnesty and gifts to key officials, Amasis secured the throne.
2. **Greek Connections**: Amasis recognized the economic advantages of Greek trade. He allowed Greeks from various city-states (especially from Ionia and the Aegean) to settle in the **Naukratis** trading post in the Delta. **Naukratis** became a hub of cultural exchange, with Greek merchants establishing temples, or "Hellenions," dedicated to their gods.
3. **Building Projects**: Amasis continued the Saite tradition of temple renovations at Memphis, Sais, and other cities.
4. **Foreign Policy**: His reign saw relative peace, though he did intervene in the Levant occasionally. Amasis formed alliances with Greek states, hoping to deter growing Persian power in the east.

Amasis's diplomatic skill brought prosperity and stability to Egypt, but an even greater threat—**the Persian Empire**—was expanding under **Cyrus the Great** and later **Cambyses II**. By the end of Amasis's reign, tension with Persia loomed large.

11.6. Prelude to Persian Invasion

11.6.1. The Rise of the Achaemenid Persians

In the mid-sixth century BCE, **Cyrus the Great** founded the **Achaemenid Empire** in Persia. Over a few decades, Persian armies conquered Lydia (in western Anatolia), Media, and Babylon. As Persian power spread westward, the Levant became a frontier zone between Persian interests and Egyptian influence.

11.6.2. Diplomatic Maneuvers and Military Preparations

Amasis sought alliances with powerful Greek city-states such as **Sparta** and **Cyrene** (in modern Libya). He provided resources, presumably hoping that joint efforts could contain Persian expansion. However, the Persian conquest of Lydia and Babylon drastically altered the balance of power in the Near East:

- **Loss of Allies**: Once Lydia fell, many Ionian Greek cities along the coast of Anatolia also submitted to Persia, reducing potential support for Egypt.
- **Shifting Mercenary Loyalties**: Greek mercenaries had to weigh lucrative Persian offers against Egyptian service. Some remained in the Delta, but others found new patrons in Asia Minor or beyond.

11.6.3. The Death of Amasis and Accession of Psamtik III

Amasis died around **526 BCE**, just as the Persian threat intensified. His successor, **Psamtik III (526–525 BCE)**, inherited a kingdom in crisis. Within a year, Persian forces under **Cambyses II** invaded, testing the Saite regime's ability to withstand the might of a vast empire.

11.7. Late Period Society on the Eve of Conquest

As the Late Period approached its climax, Egypt's social fabric displayed both continuity and new influences:

1. **Social Hierarchy**: The pharaoh and royal court in Sais wielded significant authority, supported by a bureaucracy of scribes, priests, and provincial

administrators. Mercenary generals and Greek communities held special status in the Delta, bridging Egyptian and foreign cultures.
2. **Agricultural and Economic Base**: The Nile's cyclical floods continued to sustain farming. The state collected taxes in grain and livestock, redistributed some to temples, and used the rest to support the army and officialdom. Sea trade, especially via the Greek-run port at Naukratis, enriched the treasury with tariffs and exotic goods.
3. **Local Religious Practices**: Despite the presence of foreign settlers, local Egyptians maintained temple rituals for the major gods—Amun, Ptah, Neith, Osiris, and others. Temples acted as landowners, distributing seeds, employing laborers, and hosting festivals.

Egypt under the Saite dynasty showed resilience and cultural pride, yet it stood on the threshold of a dramatic political shift. Persian power dwarfed that of earlier Near Eastern states, and Psamtik III faced the challenge of defending Egypt from a foe with extensive resources and a growing empire.

11.8. Conclusion of Chapter 11

The Late Period, initiated by the **Saite Dynasty** in 664 BCE, witnessed a renewed sense of Egyptian identity and centralized authority after centuries of fragmentation. Leaders like **Psamtik I**, **Necho II**, **Apries**, and especially **Amasis** oversaw a flourishing economy, an archaizing cultural revival, and increasing contact with the Greek world. These accomplishments testified to Egypt's enduring capacity for adaptation and self-renewal.

Yet, by the late sixth century BCE, the Persian Empire loomed as a formidable adversary. Although Amasis strove to form alliances with Greek powers to repel foreign invasion, his death and the brief rule of **Psamtik III** were overshadowed by the rapid advance of **Cambyses II**. In **525 BCE**, the Persians invaded, ending native rule and placing Egypt under a new foreign dynasty for the first time since the Hyksos many centuries earlier.

In the next chapter, **Chapter 12**, we will explore the **Persian Conquest and its Aftermath**, covering the first Persian occupation (the 27th Dynasty), subsequent brief restorations of Egyptian independence, and the second Persian occupation (the 31st Dynasty) leading up to the arrival of Alexander the Great in 332 BCE. This pivotal era reveals how Egypt endured and sometimes resisted foreign rule, preserving core traditions even in the face of profound external pressures.

CHAPTER 12

THE PERSIAN CONQUEST AND AFTERMATH

12.1. Introduction

In **525 BCE**, the Persian king **Cambyses II**, son of Cyrus the Great, led his forces into Egypt, toppling the Saite king **Psamtik III**. This event marked a new phase in the Late Period, known as the **Twenty-Seventh Dynasty** or the "First Persian Period." Although Egypt retained aspects of its traditional culture, the Achaemenid Persian kings introduced changes in administration and governance.

In the decades that followed, Egyptians staged several revolts. Briefly, native rulers (Dynasties 28, 29, and 30) regained independence, most notably under **Amyrtaeus** and the final strong pharaohs of the Thirtieth Dynasty. But in **343 BCE**, a second Persian invasion reasserted foreign control (the Thirty-First Dynasty). It was only in **332 BCE**, when **Alexander the Great** defeated Persian armies, that Persian rule in Egypt ended for good.

This chapter covers Egypt's experience under Persian domination, the temporary restorations of native rule, and the final Persian occupation—an era of upheaval and resilience that concluded the Late Period.

12.2. The First Persian Period (Twenty-Seventh Dynasty, 525–404 BCE)

12.2.1. Cambyses II (525–522 BCE) and the Conquest of Egypt

Upon his father's death, Cambyses II inherited the vast Achaemenid Empire, which already stretched from the Indus Valley to Asia Minor. Eager to expand into Africa, he crossed the Sinai with a large army, aided by local tribes and possibly Greek mercenaries who shifted loyalty after Amasis died.

1. **Battle of Pelusium**: Near the eastern Delta, Persian forces clashed with Psamtik III's army in **525 BCE**. Persian tactics and superior numbers prevailed.

2. **Capture of Memphis**: After Pelusium fell, Cambyses marched to Memphis, where Psamtik III was captured. The conquest was essentially complete; much of the country surrendered without further major resistance.
3. **Policies Toward Egyptian Temples**: Ancient sources differ. Some Greek accounts claim Cambyses showed disrespect to Egyptian religion, while other evidence suggests he supported certain temples to legitimize his rule. The truth is not fully clear, but it seems Cambyses aimed to secure cooperation from local priests and officials.

Cambyses styled himself as **Pharaoh**, adopting royal titles and acknowledging Egyptian gods. However, Persian satraps (provincial governors) held real administrative power, ensuring revenues and tribute flowed to the Persian court.

12.2.2. Darius I (522–486 BCE) and Administrative Reforms

When Cambyses died in **522 BCE**, a period of unrest followed until **Darius I** seized the Persian throne. Darius then consolidated the empire, including Egypt:

- **Satrapy System**: Egypt was governed as a **satrapy**—a province overseen by a Persian-appointed official. Many local authorities and scribes remained in place, maintaining records in Egyptian.
- **Canal Project**: Darius revived the idea of a canal linking the Nile to the Red Sea (the so-called "Canal of the Pharaohs"). Inscriptions celebrating this achievement can be found near modern Suez.
- **Respect for Temples**: Darius financed temple restorations, such as work on the Temple of Hibis in the Kharga Oasis. By supporting local cults, he hoped to reduce resistance and gain loyalty from priests who held significant influence.

Despite these pragmatic policies, many Egyptians saw Persian rule as foreign domination. Tax burdens and the presence of a Persian military garrison fueled local resentment.

12.2.3. Xerxes and Later Persian Kings of the 27th Dynasty

Xerxes I (486–465 BCE) succeeded Darius I. Engaged in wars with Greece (the Greco-Persian Wars), Xerxes paid relatively less attention to Egypt. Several revolts took place, reflecting local dissatisfaction:

- **Revolts under Xerxes and Artaxerxes I**: Egyptian rebels joined or found inspiration from other uprisings in the empire. Some local Delta lords claimed pharaonic titles, though these revolts were typically short-lived.
- **High Taxes and Forced Labor**: Persian authorities demanded tribute for empire-wide campaigns. Workers from Egypt were conscripted for large building projects, increasing strain on farmers and craftsmen.
- **Partial Autonomy**: Some local temples and regional officials still functioned with minimal interference, so long as they paid dues and stayed loyal.

The 27th Dynasty ended around **404 BCE** when Egyptian rebels finally expelled the Persian administration.

12.3. The Interim Dynasties: 28, 29, and 30 (404–343 BCE)

After driving out the Persians, Egyptians experienced nearly six decades of native rule under the **Twenty-Eighth, Twenty-Ninth,** and **Thirtieth Dynasties**. This interval reflects a desperate effort to maintain independence amid ongoing threats from Persia.

12.3.1. Amyrtaeus (28th Dynasty, 404–399 BCE)

- **Amyrtaeus of Sais** led the successful revolt against the Persians. He declared himself pharaoh, forming the short-lived **Twenty-Eighth Dynasty**.
- **Limited Achievements**: Few records survive, but it appears that Amyrtaeus spent much of his reign fending off Persian attempts to recapture the Delta.
- **End of Dynasty**: After five or six years, internal strife or rival claimants led to the demise of this line, ushering in the Twenty-Ninth Dynasty.

12.3.2. The Twenty-Ninth Dynasty (399–380 BCE)

Rulers of this dynasty, such as **Nepherites I** and **Akoris**, governed from **Mendes** in the Delta:

- **Foreign Alliances**: They tried to form alliances with Greek city-states to deter Persian reconquest. This mirrored the Saite approach but faced a mightier Persia than before.

- **Temple Construction**: Continuing the tradition of legitimizing rule through building, the Twenty-Ninth Dynasty sponsored projects at sites like **Philae** and **Abydos**. However, resources were limited, and the threat of invasion never abated.

Infighting and shifting loyalties weakened the Twenty-Ninth Dynasty, paving the way for a new line to emerge.

12.3.3. The Thirtieth Dynasty (380–343 BCE)

The **Thirtieth Dynasty** originated with **Nectanebo I** (Nakhtnebef), who seized power around **380 BCE**. This was the last fully native dynasty to hold Egypt until the modern era. They are notable for:

1. **Nectanebo I (380–362 BCE)**:
    - Successfully repelled at least one Persian invasion attempt.
    - Promoted large-scale temple building, including major additions at Karnak.
    - Allied with Greek mercenaries, some from Athens or other city-states, to bolster defenses.
2. **Teos (Djedhor, 362–360 BCE)**:
    - Reign marred by internal conflict and Greek political involvements. He was deposed by his nephew.
3. **Nectanebo II (360–343 BCE)**:
    - Known for an ambitious building program, renovating temples in Memphis, Heliopolis, and Karnak.
    - Patron of the arts, continuing the archaizing style.
    - His reign ended in defeat when the Persian king **Artaxerxes III** invaded in **343 BCE**, forcing Nectanebo II to flee to Nubia. He was the last native Egyptian to rule as pharaoh.

Under these Thirtieth Dynasty kings, Egypt momentarily recaptured the grandeur of past ages, but Persian resurgence proved insurmountable.

12.4. The Second Persian Period (Thirty-First Dynasty, 343–332 BCE)

With **Artaxerxes III**'s successful invasion, a second Persian occupation (the **Thirty-First Dynasty**) began. This time, Persian rule was more oppressive and short-lived.

12.4.1. Artaxerxes III (343–338 BCE)

- **Harsh Measures**: Ancient accounts suggest a harsher approach than the earlier Persian kings, possibly including punishment for rebels and heavy taxation to prevent future uprisings.
- **Destruction of Temples**: Some sources claim Artaxerxes III tore down fortifications and robbed temples. While there is debate, the general impression is that local populations suffered more.
- **Revolt and Chaos**: Frequent rebellions flared, though none succeeded in expelling the Persians again.

12.4.2. Artaxerxes IV and Darius III

- **Artaxerxes IV (338–336 BCE)**: His short reign was overshadowed by internal Persian court intrigues.
- **Darius III (336–330 BCE)**: Found himself battling the rising Macedonian power led by **Alexander the Great**. Persian resources were stretched thin across multiple fronts, including those in Anatolia and Mesopotamia.

By **332 BCE**, Alexander's forces marched into Egypt after defeating Persian armies in the eastern Mediterranean. Many Egyptians, resenting Persian rule, welcomed Alexander as a liberator. The surrender of Persian satraps sealed the end of the Thirty-First Dynasty and concluded the Late Period, ushering in the **Greco-Roman Period** in Egypt.

12.5. Administration and Society Under Persian Rule

During both the Twenty-Seventh and Thirty-First Dynasties, Persian rulers adapted Egyptian administration to fit their imperial model:

1. **Satrapy Status**: A Persian satrap governed on behalf of the Great King, supported by a network of smaller officials—some Persian, some local Egyptian. Taxes in grain, gold, and labor contributed to Persian war efforts.
2. **Local Elites**: Temple priests retained influence by managing religious life and local judicial matters. Often, they had to negotiate with satraps to protect temple lands.
3. **Army and Garrison Towns**: Persian and mercenary troops stationed in key cities, such as Memphis and Pelusium, to quell rebellion. This presence sometimes stifled local autonomy.

Society in Persian-ruled Egypt varied by region. The Delta, closest to the foreign center, felt stronger imperial control, while distant towns in Upper Egypt had more space for local affairs, so long as they paid taxes and avoided open revolt.

12.6. Cultural and Religious Continuities

Despite foreign conquest, traditional Egyptian religion persisted:

- **Temple Cults**: Even Persian kings, when seeking acceptance, made offerings to Egyptian gods. Darius I famously left inscriptions praising local deities.
- **Funerary Practices**: Egyptians continued mummification, tomb building, and the production of funerary goods.
- **Archaizing Art**: Sculptors in the local tradition still produced statues of officials and priests wearing archaic-style clothing, reaffirming ties to the Old Kingdom or Middle Kingdom.

Many Egyptians regarded the Persians as overlords but not as legitimate heirs to pharaonic tradition. Nonetheless, some scribes and artists cooperated with Persian authorities to maintain an administrative framework.

12.7. Political and Military Struggles Against Persia

Throughout the first Persian period, pockets of resistance occasionally flared:

- **Egyptian Revolts**: Local leaders in the Delta or Upper Egypt would declare themselves pharaoh, raising armies with Greek mercenaries or neighboring states' support.
- **Greek Alliances**: Some revolts coincided with Greek city-states' wars against Persia, especially during the classical era in Greece (5th century BCE). However, coordination across such distances was tenuous.
- **Temporary Independence**: The success of Amyrtaeus and the subsequent dynasties (28, 29, 30) proved that the Persians could be expelled. Yet these triumphs required bold leadership, foreign alliances, and a moment of Persian weakness.

The repeated back-and-forth pattern—Persian occupation, rebellion, local rule, and Persian reconquest—shows Egypt's determination to shake off foreign domination, but also the empire's sheer power.

12.8. The Final Egyptian Pharaoh: Nectanebo II

The last significant phase of native rule came under **Nectanebo II**, who reigned from **360 to 343 BCE**. During his 17-year reign:

1. **Major Temple Projects**: He completed or expanded temples at Philae, Edfu, and other sites, carving reliefs that celebrated ancient myths and reaffirmed his role as a pious king.
2. **Diplomatic and Military Efforts**: Nectanebo II hired Greek mercenaries, forging alliances with some Greek city-states. But internal Greek conflicts (such as disputes among major polis powers) weakened the potential for strong, unified support.
3. **Final Defeat**: In **343 BCE**, the Persian king Artaxerxes III invaded. After battles in the Delta, Nectanebo II withdrew to Upper Egypt, then fled to Nubia or other safe regions. His exile ended the last native pharaonic dynasty.

Nectanebo II left a lasting cultural legacy: many later Egyptians and even foreign rulers looked back to his reign as a time of religious dedication, artistic achievement, and patriotic fervor.

12.9. The Arrival of Alexander the Great (332 BCE)

The second Persian domination was short. Barely a decade later, **Alexander the Great** defeated the Persian forces at Issus and continued his campaign into Syria and Palestine. By **332 BCE**, Alexander entered Egypt unopposed. Locals—disillusioned with Persian rule—often welcomed him as a liberator.

Alexander paid homage at the Temple of Ptah in Memphis and traveled to the Siwa Oasis to consult the Oracle of Amun, an act echoing the ancient tradition of kings seeking divine legitimacy. This event effectively ended the Late Period, transitioning Egypt into the **Greco-Roman Period** under Macedonian—and later Ptolemaic—control.

12.10. Legacy of the Persian Conquest and Aftermath

Despite the turbulence of Persian invasions and the fleeting revivals of native rule, Egypt maintained its cultural core:

- **Religious Continuity**: Temple building and the worship of ancient deities persisted, even as foreign kings claimed titles like "Pharaoh."
- **Administrative Adaptations**: Under Persian rule, Egyptian scribes learned to navigate imperial demands. Basic structures from the pharaonic bureaucracy continued, adapted to satrap administration.
- **Art and Architecture**: When native dynasties briefly returned, they produced a final flourish of grand temple construction, especially under Nectanebo II.
- **Prelude to Hellenistic Egypt**: The Greek presence, already established at Naukratis, accelerated under Alexander and the subsequent Ptolemaic Dynasty. Many Egyptians later adapted to Hellenistic influences while retaining local customs, forming a unique blend of cultures.

With Alexander's conquest, a new chapter began—one in which Greek language, art, and governance would intermingle with millennia-old Egyptian traditions. The Persians left behind an administrative precedent, but after 332 BCE, control of Egypt passed definitively into the hands of Macedonian and then Roman rulers.

12.11. Conclusion of Chapter 12

The **Persian Conquest** of Egypt in 525 BCE reshaped the Late Period. While the Saite Dynasty attempted to uphold native traditions and political autonomy, it could not match the Achaemenid Empire's might. The first Persian occupation under Cambyses and Darius introduced new administrative methods but also fueled Egyptian resentment. Intermittent revolts led to a series of short native dynasties (28, 29, 30) that valiantly tried to restore full independence. The final native pharaoh, **Nectanebo II**, personified Egypt's last stand against foreign rule, before succumbing to a renewed Persian invasion in 343 BCE.

This second period of Persian domination ended abruptly when **Alexander the Great** liberated Egypt from Persian control in **332 BCE**. That moment concluded the Late Period and heralded the start of the **Greco-Roman Period**, when Egypt would come under Macedonian (Ptolemaic) rule and later Roman authority.

CHAPTER 13

THE GRECO-ROMAN PERIOD

13.1. Introduction to the Greco-Roman Period (332 BCE – 642 CE)

The **Greco-Roman Period** of Egyptian history begins with **Alexander the Great's** arrival in **332 BCE** and extends until the Arab Conquest in **642 CE** (though the final centuries of Roman rule overlap with the spread of Christianity and will be discussed in the next chapter). During these nearly one thousand years, two successive foreign powers—the **Macedonian (or Greek) Ptolemaic dynasty** followed by **Roman rule**—shaped Egypt's politics, economy, culture, and religion in far-reaching ways.

Under Alexander's successors, the **Ptolemies**, Egypt became a Greek-speaking kingdom centered in **Alexandria**, a new cosmopolitan city that quickly became a beacon of learning and trade. The cultural blending of Greek and Egyptian elements produced distinctive art, architecture, and religious practices that resonated across the Mediterranean world. Later, when **Rome** incorporated Egypt into its empire in **30 BCE**, the country served as a vital source of grain and wealth for the capital. Roman emperors maintained much of the administrative framework that the Ptolemies had established, but they also introduced new legal and social structures.

In this chapter, we explore Egypt's changing fortunes under Greek and Roman administrations, focusing on the transformation of its cities, the interplay of cultures, the continued worship of traditional deities, and the emergence of new religious and intellectual currents. By the time Arab armies arrived in the 7th century CE, Egypt had become a key province of the Eastern Roman (Byzantine) Empire, with Christian faith on the rise—leading us into the subject of **Christian Egypt** covered in the next chapter.

13.2. The Macedonian Conquest: Alexander the Great (332–323 BCE)

13.2.1. Alexander's Entry into Egypt

When **Alexander the Great** defeated Persian forces at Issus and advanced through the Levant, Egypt—exhausted by the harsh rule of the second Persian occupation—offered little resistance. In **332 BCE**, the Persian satrap handed over authority without a significant battle, and Alexander was welcomed as a liberator. He traveled to **Memphis**, the ancient capital, performing ceremonial rites to establish legitimacy as pharaoh in the eyes of both Egyptian priests and the general population.

13.2.2. Founding of Alexandria

One of Alexander's lasting legacies was the establishment of the city of **Alexandria** on Egypt's Mediterranean coast. According to tradition, Alexander personally marked out the boundaries. Key features of early Alexandria included:

- **Strategic Port**: Natural harbors connected to the Nile Delta, ideal for maritime trade.
- **Urban Planning**: Greek-style grid of streets, grand avenues, and designated areas for temples and public buildings.
- **Cosmopolitan Character**: Alexandria soon attracted settlers from Greece, Asia Minor, Phoenicia, and beyond, forming a diverse population.

Alexander also traveled to the **Siwa Oasis** to consult the oracle of Amun, seeking confirmation of his semi-divine status. This act further fused Greek notions of divine kingship with Egyptian traditions of pharaonic divinity.

13.2.3. Aftermath of Alexander's Death

Alexander died in **323 BCE** in Babylon, leaving no adult heir. His generals, known as the **Diadochi**, carved up the empire. Egypt fell to **Ptolemy**, one of Alexander's trusted commanders. Over the next decades, Ptolemy consolidated his hold on Egypt, inaugurating the **Ptolemaic Dynasty**—the most enduring Hellenistic state formed out of Alexander's conquests.

13.3. The Ptolemaic Dynasty (323–30 BCE)

13.3.1. Ptolemy I Soter and the Foundation of the Ptolemaic Kingdom

Ptolemy I Soter (r. 305–285 BCE) declared himself king around **305 BCE**, establishing a royal line based in Alexandria. Key steps in consolidating power included:

- **Securing Borders**: He defended Egypt against rival Hellenistic rulers, including Seleucus in the Near East and Antigonus in Asia Minor.
- **Administration**: Ptolemy and his successors blended Greek administrative methods with local Egyptian bureaucracy. Officials documented transactions in Greek and demotic Egyptian scripts, ensuring cooperation between Greek elites and indigenous scribes.
- **Religious Policy**: Ptolemy recognized that the priesthood was central to Egyptian society. He supported the rebuilding of temples and offered donations to major cult centers, winning favor among Egyptian priests.

13.3.2. Economic Organization and Land Management

The Ptolemies meticulously organized Egypt's agriculture to maximize revenue. Major policies:

1. **State Control of Agriculture**: Much of the arable land was royal domain. Farmers paid taxes in grain, fruit, or other produce.
2. **Irrigation Projects**: Maintaining and expanding canal networks ensured stable harvests.
3. **State Monopolies**: Ptolemies often set state monopolies on goods like oil, papyrus, or beer, using these revenues to fund the royal court and military.

This economic system proved highly profitable, enabling the Ptolemies to maintain large armies and erect monumental buildings throughout the kingdom.

13.3.3. Cultural Synthesis and the Deification of Rulers

The Ptolemies nurtured a **fusion** of Greek and Egyptian cultures:

- **Deified Rulers**: Ptolemaic kings adopted pharaonic titles and were sometimes portrayed in Egyptian iconography, while also encouraging Greek civic cults that honored them as gods.
- **Temples and Syncretic Deities**: Greek influence merged with Egyptian religious imagery. A prime example is **Serapis**, a deity combining attributes of the Egyptian god Osiris-Apis and Greek gods like Zeus or Hades.
- **Patronage of Scholarship**: The **Library of Alexandria** and the **Mouseion** (House of the Muses) became leading centers of Greek learning, gathering

scholars, philosophers, and scientists from across the Mediterranean world.

13.3.4. Notable Ptolemaic Rulers

- **Ptolemy II Philadelphus (285–246 BCE)**: Strengthened Alexandria's cultural prominence; built the **Pharos** (lighthouse), one of the Seven Wonders of the Ancient World.
- **Ptolemy III Euergetes (246–222 BCE)**: Expanded Egyptian control briefly into parts of the Near East; known for a prosperous reign.
- **Ptolemy IV Philopator, Ptolemy V Epiphanes**, and others: Internal court intrigues, growing Roman influence, and economic strain began to weaken the dynasty over time.
- **Cleopatra VII (51–30 BCE)**: The last active ruler of the Ptolemaic Kingdom, famous for her alliances with Roman leaders **Julius Caesar** and **Mark Antony**. Her defeat by **Octavian** (the future Augustus) in **30 BCE** effectively ended Ptolemaic rule and brought Egypt under direct Roman control.

13.4. Roman Egypt (30 BCE – 4th Century CE)

13.4.1. The Establishment of Roman Rule

After Cleopatra and Mark Antony's defeat at the **Battle of Actium** (31 BCE), **Octavian** annexed Egypt as a personal province in **30 BCE**. This direct annexation meant:

- **Prefect of Egypt**: A Roman official (equestrian rank) governed Egypt in the emperor's name. Senators were barred from entering Egypt without permission, underscoring the emperor's exclusive authority.
- **Key Grain Supply**: Rome relied heavily on Egyptian grain to feed the urban population. The province's security and stability were vital to the empire.
- **Social Hierarchy**: Romans, Greek-speaking elites (descended from Ptolemaic settlers), and indigenous Egyptians coexisted under a layered system of privileges, taxes, and legal statuses.

13.4.2. Economic Continuities and New Developments

The Romans inherited a sophisticated agricultural system that they maintained and sometimes expanded:

1. **Irrigation and Harvests**: The Roman prefect ensured that canals, dikes, and basin irrigation remained functional.
2. **Taxes and Exports**: A portion of each year's grain harvest was shipped to Rome or other parts of the empire. Exports also included flax, papyrus, and glassware.
3. **Landholdings**: Large estates persisted under wealthy Romans or Hellenized local nobility. Small farmers, many of whom were native Egyptians, continued to live in village communities, paying taxes to local officials.

13.4.3. Administration and Society

Under Roman governance:

- **Local Administration**: Egyptian towns had councils called **boule** (in Greek), run by local notables responsible for tax collection and municipal services.
- **Legal Pluralism**: Roman law governed Roman citizens and certain elite groups, while native Egyptians used a mixture of Egyptian and Greek legal traditions. Over time, more Egyptians sought the privilege of Roman citizenship, which brought tax exemptions or reduced burdens.
- **Military Garrisons**: Roman legions were stationed at strategic sites—particularly along the southern frontier (Nubia) and near the desert routes—to protect trade and guard against incursions.

13.4.4. Cultural and Religious Life under Rome

Roman emperors often presented themselves as successors to the pharaohs. They made offerings in Egyptian temples and erected or restored shrines. Meanwhile:

- **Greco-Roman Deities**: Worship of Isis, Anubis, and other Egyptian gods spread throughout the empire, especially among Greeks and Romans fascinated by the mystique of Egyptian religion. The cult of **Isis** became especially popular in Rome itself.

- **Artistic Styles**: Funerary portraits found in the Faiyum region (the so-called "Faiyum mummy portraits") combined Roman portrait techniques (realistic encaustic painting) with traditional Egyptian burial practices (mummies placed in painted cartonnage).
- **Intellectual Centers**: Alexandria remained a hub of scholarship, with philosophers, mathematicians, and astronomers continuing the Hellenistic traditions. Notable figures such as **Claudius Ptolemy** (the geographer-astronomer) worked in Roman Alexandria.

Despite relative prosperity, tensions arose periodically—local rebellions, disputes over taxes, and new religious movements (including early Christianity) would later challenge imperial authority.

13.5. Shifting Dynamics in the Later Roman Empire

By the 3rd century CE, the Roman Empire faced multiple crises—economic hardships, external invasions, and internal power struggles. Egypt was not immune:

13.5.1. Economic Strain and Provincial Reforms

- **Inflation and Debased Coinage**: Roman emperors often debased currency to fund wars, causing price instability. Egyptian farmers and traders suffered from devaluation and heavy taxation.
- **Administrative Reorganization**: Under **Diocletian** (late 3rd–early 4th century CE), the empire was divided into smaller provinces. Egypt's older administrative model was updated, though the prefect still oversaw vital grain shipments. Diocletian also imposed new edicts on pricing and taxation, attempting to stabilize the empire's economy.

13.5.2. Early Christianity in Roman Egypt

Christianity spread gradually, first among Greek-speaking communities in Alexandria, then into local Egyptian populations. By the 4th century, Christian believers formed a significant minority, laying the groundwork for the **Coptic Church** that would flourish later. We will explore this in detail in the next chapter.

13.5.3. Declining Central Control

As Roman authority waned, the province experienced sporadic uprisings. However, Roman armies generally maintained order in urban centers, especially Alexandria, which remained a crucial port and commercial city. Many changes in the 4th century CE—particularly the Christianization of the empire under Emperor Constantine—reshaped local religious life.

13.6. The Byzantine (Eastern Roman) Phase (4th–7th Centuries CE)

With the empire's division into East and West, Egypt fell under the **Eastern Roman Empire** (commonly called **Byzantine**). Key developments:

1. **Continued Grain Exports**: Constantinople relied heavily on Egyptian grain shipments, mirroring Rome's earlier dependence.
2. **Christian Dominance**: The state-endorsed Christian Church gained power. Egyptian monasticism emerged in deserts near the Nile, a movement that influenced Christian practice across the empire.
3. **Cultural Shifts**: Greek remained the language of administration, but the Egyptian (Coptic) language took on new significance in church contexts.

By the early 7th century, Persian armies (under the Sasanian Empire) briefly occupied parts of Egypt, highlighting the vulnerability of Byzantine control. Soon after, Arab forces arrived, leading to a new chapter in Egyptian history.

13.7. Daily Life and Social Transformations in the Greco-Roman Period

Despite changes in leadership, many aspects of everyday life showed continuity:

- **Village Life**: Most Egyptians continued to farm, raise livestock, and practice local crafts. Family structures and seasonal rhythms (planting, harvesting) followed the Nile flood cycles.
- **Towns and Cities**: The introduction of Greek-style institutions (gymnasia, theaters, and boule) altered urban lifestyles, especially among Greek-speaking elites who enjoyed privileges like reduced taxes. Romans later integrated these Greek civic institutions into imperial structures.
- **Status and Ethnicity**: Under Ptolemaic rule, Greeks held the highest social standing. Under Rome, Roman citizens (including some Greek elites who obtained citizenship) enjoyed legal and tax advantages. Native Egyptians formed the bulk of the population, often bearing heavier fiscal

burdens. Over time, intermarriage blurred ethnic lines, and many Egyptians adopted Greek or Latin names.

13.8. Religion and Art in a Multi-Cultural Context

Egypt's cultural mosaic became increasingly complex:

1. **Traditional Deities**: Large temples, such as those at Edfu, Dendera, and Philae, received Ptolemaic and Roman patronage. These constructions continued the style of earlier pharaonic eras, featuring hieroglyphic inscriptions and colossal stone gateways (pylons).
2. **New Deities and Mysteries**: Cults like that of **Serapis** and **Isis** appealed to a broad audience—Egyptians, Greeks, and other foreigners—offering mystical initiation rites and promises of an afterlife.
3. **Artistic Fusion**: Sculptures of Ptolemaic rulers often showed them in Greek dress but with pharaonic regalia. Roman-era funerary art, such as the Faiyum portraits, combined realistic Roman portraiture with Egyptian burial traditions (wrapping mummies, placing them in tombs).

This melding of styles and beliefs made Egypt a cultural crossroads where pharaonic heritage coexisted with Hellenistic and Roman innovations.

13.9. Intellectual Life and Scholarship: The Alexandrian Tradition

Alexandria stood at the forefront of Greco-Roman intellectual life:

- **Library of Alexandria**: Though its exact size and fate are debated, it was widely regarded as the largest library of the ancient world, housing texts on philosophy, mathematics, astronomy, geography, medicine, and more.
- **Famous Scholars**:
    - **Euclid** (3rd century BCE), known for his foundational work in geometry.
    - **Archimedes** (briefly associated with Alexandria), advanced mathematical physics.
    - **Eratosthenes** (3rd century BCE), measured the Earth's circumference.
    - **Claudius Ptolemy** (2nd century CE), compiled astronomical works that influenced science until the Renaissance.

- **Medical Advances**: Anatomists studied the human body using methods gleaned from earlier Egyptian embalming practices, achieving breakthroughs in medicine and surgery.

Although some Greek intellectuals viewed Egypt's ancient lore with curiosity and awe, the actual continuity of older Egyptian scientific traditions can be difficult to trace, as Greek replaced hieroglyphic and demotic in many scholarly domains. Still, certain Egyptian religious and magical texts continued to be copied and studied in temple schools until well into the Roman period.

13.10. Political Unrest and Resistance Movements

While the Greco-Roman period saw economic and cultural prosperity, not all Egyptians accepted foreign rule passively:

1. **Rebellions**: In the Ptolemaic era, uprisings sometimes centered in Upper Egypt, where local princes declared themselves pharaoh. These revolts occurred especially during weaker reigns or dynastic disputes in Alexandria.
2. **Banditry**: Under the Romans, some peasant communities resorted to banditry in protest against high taxes or administrative injustices. Roman prefects dispatched troops to quell these uprisings.
3. **Religious Factions**: Tensions between traditional Egyptian priesthoods and the newly favored cults (Greek or Roman) occasionally erupted, especially if temple land allocations changed or if new taxes threatened local economies.

Despite these episodes, the foreign regimes effectively maintained control, ensuring the steady flow of tax revenue and grain exports.

13.11. Transition to Christian Egypt

By the 4th century CE, Christianity was no longer a small minority faith. The emperor **Constantine** (early 4th century) legalized Christianity across the empire, and soon after, it gained official preference. In Egypt:

- **Bishoprics**: Cities like Alexandria became centers of Christian theological debate, shaping doctrines that influenced the wider Mediterranean world.

- **Decline of Traditional Temples**: Government support shifted to churches, and some pagan temples lost patrons. By the early 5th century, decrees from Constantinople suppressed or repurposed pagan sites.
- **Emergence of Monasticism**: The Egyptian deserts became famous for anchorites (hermits) and monastic communities. Figures like **Anthony the Great** (3rd–4th century CE) played pivotal roles, inspiring Christian ascetic traditions far beyond Egypt.

This gradual transformation from a polytheistic society to a predominantly Christian one will be the central focus of the next chapter, covering the "**Christian Egypt and the Coptic Era.**"

13.12. Conclusion of Chapter 13

The **Greco-Roman Period** (332 BCE – 642 CE) introduced profound changes to Egypt while preserving many core traditions. The **Ptolemies** created a unique fusion of Greek and Egyptian customs, ruling from Alexandria, fostering scholarship, and supporting local priesthoods. Their kingdom remained wealthy and influential for three centuries but gradually succumbed to internal strife and Roman pressure.

With **Cleopatra VII's** defeat in **30 BCE**, Rome turned Egypt into a centrally managed province. Although Roman administration was strict, the economy thrived on grain exports, and cultural life continued to flourish, especially in Alexandria. Over time, Christianity emerged as a transformative force, altering religious landscapes and gradually diminishing the once-prominent role of Egyptian temples and priesthoods. By the 7th century CE, the Eastern Roman (Byzantine) Empire faced challenges from within and without, paving the way for the Arab Conquest of Egypt in **642 CE**.

In the next chapter, **Chapter 14**, we focus on **Christian Egypt and the Coptic Era**, examining how Christian beliefs spread throughout the country, how they merged with or replaced older religious practices, and how the Egyptian Church established a distinct identity that endures to this day.

CHAPTER 14

CHRISTIAN EGYPT AND THE COPTIC ERA

14.1. Introduction to Christian Egypt (1st–7th Centuries CE)

The story of **Christian Egypt** begins in the Roman period, as the new faith, originating in Judea, reached Alexandria and other Egyptian cities during the 1st century CE. Over the following centuries, Christianity transitioned from a minority religion facing periodic persecution to the dominant faith of the region, supported by imperial edicts and the rising influence of the Church hierarchy.

The **Coptic Era** specifically refers to the development of Christianity in Egypt in its own unique form, with a distinct language (Coptic), liturgy, and traditions that emerged out of the interaction between ancient Egyptian culture and Christian beliefs. By the time the Arab armies arrived in 642 CE, the majority of Egyptians were affiliated with the **Coptic Church**, which continued under Islamic rule with varying degrees of autonomy and pressure.

This chapter covers the spread of Christianity in Egypt, the role of Alexandria as a theological center, the formation of monasticism in the Egyptian deserts, and the religious debates that shaped the Coptic identity. We conclude by examining how these transformations prepared Egypt for the transition into the **Arab Conquest** and the subsequent changes in centuries to come.

14.2. The Beginnings of Christianity in Egypt

14.2.1. Early Christian Communities in Alexandria

Legend credits **Saint Mark** with bringing Christianity to Alexandria in the mid-1st century CE, establishing a small community of converts. While historical details are scarce, it is clear that:

- **Alexandria's Cosmopolitan Nature**: Home to Jews, Greeks, Romans, and other groups, the city was fertile ground for new ideas and doctrines.
- **Greek-Speaking Church**: In its earliest phase, Christian worship in Alexandria likely used Greek for liturgy and scripture, reflecting the city's Hellenistic culture.

14.2.2. Expansion to Other Regions

From Alexandria, Christianity gradually spread to other Egyptian cities and rural areas, though the process took centuries:

- **Urban Centers**: Faiyum, Oxyrhynchus, and Hermopolis had growing Christian populations by the 3rd and 4th centuries. Archaeological finds, such as papyri and ostraca, reveal Christian letters, homilies, and administrative texts.
- **Resistance and Syncretism**: Some Egyptians continued to observe the old gods, leading to a phase of religious competition. In some cases, Christian and pagan elements blended temporarily, with new converts retaining certain older customs.

14.3. Roman Persecution and Imperial Acceptance

14.3.1. Persecutions under Various Emperors

Though early Christianity spread quietly, Roman authorities sometimes viewed Christians with suspicion:

- **Decius (249–251 CE)** and **Diocletian (284–305 CE)**: Issued edicts demanding public sacrifice to Roman gods. Christians who refused faced arrest, confiscation of property, and sometimes execution. In Egypt, local officials carried out these edicts, leading to martyrdom accounts.
- **Martyrs of Alexandria**: Saints like **Catherine of Alexandria** are remembered in Christian tradition, though historical records are mixed. Still, stories of steadfast faith under persecution inspired later generations.

14.3.2. Constantine and the Edict of Milan (313 CE)

When **Constantine** became emperor in the early 4th century, he issued the **Edict of Milan** (313 CE), granting religious tolerance to Christians. Over the next decades:

- **Imperial Support**: Churches received state funding and property. Persecutions ended.

- **Shift in Popular Devotion**: Many Egyptians took advantage of the new freedoms, converting to Christianity or openly displaying their Christian faith.

By the end of the 4th century, **Theodosius I** declared Christianity the empire's official religion, prompting the systematic closure or repurposing of many pagan temples throughout Egypt.

14.4. The Arian Controversy and the Council of Nicaea (325 CE)

14.4.1. Alexandrian Theologians and Christological Debates

Alexandria emerged as a major center of Christian theology. Intellectuals like **Origen** (3rd century) and **Athanasius** (4th century) shaped key doctrines. However, disputes about the nature of Christ caused deep rifts:

- **Arius**, an Alexandrian priest, taught that the Son was not co-eternal with the Father. This stance challenged the idea of Christ's full divinity.
- **Bishop Alexander of Alexandria** and his successor **Athanasius** condemned Arius, sparking controversy throughout the Christian world.

14.4.2. Council of Nicaea (325 CE)

The emperor Constantine convened the **Council of Nicaea** to resolve the Arian dispute. The Council upheld the position that Christ was "of one substance" (homoousios) with the Father. However:

- **Arian Influence Remained**: Even after Nicaea, many bishops and emperors leaned toward Arian or semi-Arian interpretations. Athanasius spent years exiled due to imperial disfavor.
- **Continued Divisions**: The conflict foreshadowed further theological schisms, which would later shape the **Coptic Church's** identity.

14.5. Rise of Monasticism in Egypt

Egypt played a pivotal role in Christian monastic traditions:

14.5.1. The Desert Fathers

Individuals like **Saint Anthony the Great** (c. 251–356 CE) withdrew to remote desert locations to live in prayer and asceticism. Over time, devotees gathered near them, seeking spiritual guidance:

- **Anchoritic Monasticism**: Hermits lived alone or in small groups, practicing extreme austerities.
- **Influence Abroad**: Stories of Anthony and others reached the wider Christian world, encouraging monastic movements in Palestine, Syria, and later in the Latin West.

14.5.2. Pachomius and Communal Monasticism

Saint Pachomius (c. 292–348 CE) founded **cenobitic** monasteries, where monks lived in a structured community:

- **Regulated Lifestyle**: Shared work, prayer, and communal meals under an abbot.
- **Written Rule**: Pachomius established guidelines that influenced future monastic orders, including those in Europe.
- **Expansion**: Numerous monasteries formed along the Nile, turning the Egyptian deserts into spiritual enclaves. Many monasteries, like those in **Wadi Natrun** (Scetis), remained influential for centuries.

Monasticism became a hallmark of Egyptian Christian identity, attracting pilgrims from across the empire. It also provided a space for biblical scholarship and the copying of sacred texts.

14.6. The Coptic Church and Its Language

14.6.1. Development of the Coptic Script

As Christianity spread among native Egyptians, they needed a written form of their own language for liturgy and scripture. **Coptic** emerged by merging the Greek alphabet with a few demotic signs for sounds not found in Greek. Over time:

- **Scriptural Translations**: The Bible was translated into Coptic, enabling common people to understand sermons and read religious texts.

- **Literary Works**: Sermons, hagiographies, and monastic rules were composed in Coptic, fostering a rich Christian literature.
- **Everyday Use**: Although Greek remained important for administration, Coptic became the primary medium of religious and daily communication for many Egyptian Christians.

14.6.2. Ecclesiastical Structure

The **Patriarch (Pope) of Alexandria** led the Egyptian Church. While early patriarchs were often Greek-speaking, the Church's base increasingly included Egyptian clergy. Alexandria's patriarch gained prestige because of the city's historical significance and the theological scholarship associated with it.

14.7. The Chalcedonian Schism and the Miaphysite Position

14.7.1. Council of Chalcedon (451 CE)

Theological disputes about Christ's nature continued after Nicaea. At the **Council of Chalcedon** in 451 CE, the empire endorsed the doctrine that Christ possessed two natures—divine and human—united in one person. However, many Egyptian bishops rejected this conclusion:

- **Miaphysite Position**: Egyptian Christians (and some in Syria) held that Christ's divine and human natures were united in one nature (mia physis), without separation or confusion. They saw the Chalcedonian "two natures" teaching as an overemphasis on division.
- **Formation of the Coptic Orthodox Church**: As a result, the Egyptian Church broke communion with the imperial Church, forming its own distinct tradition. This theological stance shaped Egyptian Christian identity and is still held by the Coptic Orthodox Church today.

14.7.2. Political and Cultural Consequences

Roman (later Byzantine) emperors often supported Chalcedonian patriarchs in Alexandria, while the majority of Egyptian Christians favored Miaphysite leaders. This rift:

- **Fostered Local Solidarity**: Many Egyptians came to see the Byzantine religious policy as oppressive or heretical.
- **Increased Tensions**: Imperial governors sometimes persecuted Miaphysite bishops and monks, further alienating Egyptian Christians from Constantinople's authority.

By the 6th century, the divide between Chalcedonian ("Melkite") and Miaphysite ("Coptic") Christians was deeply ingrained, affecting governance and society alike.

14.8. Daily Christian Life in Byzantine Egypt

14.8.1. Urban and Rural Congregations

Most Egyptians, now Christian, worshiped in local parish churches. Some features of daily life included:

- **Festivals and Saints' Days**: Christian feast days, such as Easter and local saint commemorations, punctuated the calendar, replacing older pagan festivals.
- **Pilgrimage**: Egyptians visited monastic centers or shrines dedicated to martyrs, forging a network of religious tourism and donations.
- **Charitable Institutions**: Churches and monasteries often provided care for orphans, widows, and the poor, expanding Christian social influence.

14.8.2. Continued Use of Temples and Shrines

While major temples to Egyptian gods had lost official state patronage, some local cults survived discreetly, merging or morphing into Christian traditions. In certain villages, the memory of old gods lingered in popular folklore, but the Church strove to channel popular devotion toward saints and biblical figures.

14.8.3. Artistic Expressions

Christian art in the Coptic era included:

- **Wall Paintings**: Church interiors, monastery walls, and shrines were decorated with biblical scenes, saints, and angels.
- **Icons and Illuminated Manuscripts**: Coptic iconography developed unique styles, showing elongated figures and vibrant colors that emphasized spiritual qualities.
- **Textiles**: Egypt was famous for linen and tapestry weaving. Christian symbols—crosses, angels, and vine motifs—appeared on clothing and church hangings, reflecting a fusion of classical and local motifs.

14.9. Political Challenges in the 6th and 7th Centuries

14.9.1. Justinian and Further Centralization

The Byzantine emperor **Justinian I** (527–565 CE) attempted to unify the empire religiously, closing pagan schools and supporting Chalcedonian bishops. This policy exacerbated tensions with Miaphysite Egyptians, seen by locals as religious oppression. Sporadic conflicts erupted, and although local revolts did not fully break Byzantine control, they heightened resentment.

14.9.2. Persian Invasion (616–629 CE)

In the early 7th century, **Sasanian Persians** under King Khosrow II invaded the Near East and briefly occupied parts of Egypt (c. 616–629 CE). This occupation eroded Byzantine power and revealed Egypt's vulnerability to foreign attack. Although Emperor Heraclius eventually drove out the Persians, the province was weakened by years of conflict, taxation, and disruption of trade.

14.9.3. The Final Days of Byzantine Egypt

By the 630s, the Eastern Roman Empire struggled to maintain security. The local population, largely Coptic and alienated by constant religious and fiscal pressures, showed limited support for Byzantine defenders. Thus, when **Arab forces** under the banner of Islam advanced toward Egypt in the early 640s, Byzantine governance lacked a strong local base.

14.10. The Arab Conquest (642 CE) and the End of Byzantine Rule

Arab armies, having subdued much of the Levant, marched into Egypt around **639–640 CE** under the commander **'Amr ibn al-'As**. Key battles and sieges (e.g., the fortress of Babylon near Memphis) led to a treaty:

- **Fall of Alexandria**: After initial peace terms, Alexandria eventually fell in **642 CE**.
- **Transition of Power**: The new rulers allowed Christian communities to remain under certain conditions, with the payment of a poll tax (jizya) in exchange for protection and limited autonomy.
- **End of the Greco-Roman Era**: Roman (Byzantine) control ended, marking a major shift in Egypt's political and cultural landscape. Although many aspects of daily life continued, the official use of Greek in administration

gradually gave way to Arabic. Church structures remained but adapted to new conditions, leading to a centuries-long story of Christian-Muslim coexistence in Egypt.

Thus, the **Coptic Era**, rooted in the transformations of the later Roman Empire, carried forward under Islamic rule, forging a unique Christian minority heritage that persists to modern times.

14.11. Legacy of Christian Egypt

The centuries of Christian dominance in Egypt left deep cultural and religious marks:

1. **Coptic Language**: Although it gradually diminished after Arabic became the language of governance, Coptic survived as a liturgical tongue, preserving a link to ancient Egyptian.
2. **Monastic Traditions**: Egyptian monasticism influenced Christian monastic practices worldwide, from Eastern Orthodox to Western Catholic orders.
3. **Art and Architecture**: Coptic churches, icons, and illuminated manuscripts display enduring stylistic traits, connecting ancient Egyptian iconography and Hellenistic influences with Christian themes.
4. **Religious Identity**: The Miaphysite belief set the Coptic Orthodox Church apart from Greek Orthodoxy and Roman Catholicism, defining Egypt's Christian community for centuries.
5. **Historical Continuity**: In Coptic Christianity, one can observe lines of continuity with pharaonic religion—such as emphasis on fasting, ritual purity, and reverence for sacred places—now channeled through a distinct Christian framework.

CHAPTER 15

THE ARAB CONQUEST OF EGYPT

15.1. Introduction to the Arab Conquest (7th Century CE)

Egypt faced major political, cultural, and religious changes when **Arab armies**, under the banner of **Islam**, advanced into the region in the early **7th century CE**. At that time, Egypt was a province of the **Byzantine Empire**, internally divided by religious disputes between the Chalcedonian imperial church and the local Coptic (Miaphysite) majority. The Persian occupation (616–629 CE) had further weakened Byzantine control, leaving the region vulnerable.

When Islamic forces led by **'Amr ibn al-'As** arrived around **639–640 CE**, they encountered a population with mixed loyalties, heavy tax burdens, and dissatisfaction with Byzantine rule. Despite pockets of resistance, the Arab armies captured key centers, culminating in the fall of **Alexandria** by **642 CE**. This event ended centuries of Greco-Roman governance and laid the foundation for **Islamic Egypt**—a transformation that shaped the country's identity, language, and administrative structures for centuries to come.

In this chapter, we explore the motivations behind the Arab campaign in Egypt, the military and diplomatic strategies that led to success, and the initial impact of Islamic governance on the predominantly Christian population. We close by examining how this period of conquest set the stage for later Islamic dynasties, leading ultimately to the **Fatimid Era**, covered in the next chapter.

15.2. The Wider Context: Rise of Islam and Regional Shifts

15.2.1. The Emergence of Islam in Arabia

Islam began in the early 7th century CE with the revelations received by the Prophet **Muhammad** (c. 570–632 CE) in the Arabian Peninsula. By the time of Muhammad's death in **632 CE**, most of Arabia recognized his spiritual and temporal authority, though challenges to the new faith persisted. The first caliphs who succeeded Muhammad consolidated this unity and expanded outward.

15.2.2. The Rashidun Caliphate and Its Conquests

The initial phase of Islamic expansion is associated with the **Rashidun ("Rightly Guided") Caliphs**: Abu Bakr (632–634), 'Umar (634–644), 'Uthman (644–656), and 'Ali (656–661). During this period:

- **Military and Religious Zeal**: Arab tribes, newly united under Islam, directed their energy outward.
- **Conquests in the Levant and Persia**: After victories against Byzantine forces at battles like **Yarmouk** (636 CE) and against the Sasanian Persians in Iraq, the caliphate turned its attention to Egypt, a rich and strategic province.

15.3. Egypt Under Byzantine Rule Just Before the Conquest

15.3.1. Provincial Administration

By the 7th century, Egypt was administered by a Byzantine governor (often titled the **dux** or **prefect**), who reported to the emperor in Constantinople. The local capital was still **Alexandria**, a major port city. Meanwhile, the countryside was divided into districts for tax collection, with the produce—particularly grain—shipped to support the imperial capital.

15.3.2. Religious Tensions

Egypt's population was mainly **Coptic** Christian, following Miaphysite beliefs. However, the imperial Church in Constantinople endorsed Chalcedonian doctrine. Disagreements led to:

- **Alienation of the Copts**: Many saw Byzantine rule as oppressive, especially when officials attempted to enforce Chalcedonian orthodoxy.
- **Periodic Persecution**: Local Miaphysite clergy or bishops faced restrictions or exile. This policy harmed relations between the central government and the bulk of the Egyptian population.

15.3.3. Economic Burdens and Military Weakness

Frequent wars (including the recent Persian occupation) depleted Byzantium's ability to defend distant provinces. Heavy taxes and forced contributions of grain strained Egyptian producers, who often resented the imperial demands. This resentment contributed to a lukewarm response when Byzantine authorities called for local support against the Arab advance.

15.4. The Arab Invasion of Egypt (639–642 CE)

15.4.1. Early Operations: 'Amr ibn al-'As

The caliph 'Umar appointed **'Amr ibn al-'As** to lead a small force into Egypt, probably around **639 CE**. 'Amr had prior commercial and diplomatic ties to the region, so he understood its political and social landscape. Initial actions:

- **Crossing of the Sinai**: Arab troops moved from Palestine into the Sinai Peninsula, capturing frontier outposts with minimal Byzantine resistance.
- **Local Communities**: Some Egyptian towns, especially in the eastern Delta, surrendered quickly, sometimes through negotiated truces promising security in exchange for taxes.

15.4.2. The Battle of Heliopolis (c. 640 CE)

One of the key confrontations occurred near **Heliopolis** (close to modern Cairo):

- **Byzantine Defenses**: The local commander likely tried to block Arab advances along the Nile. However, internal divisions and insufficient reinforcements weakened the defense.
- **Arab Victory**: The well-coordinated forces of 'Amr ibn al-'As overcame Byzantine troops, securing the path to Memphis and controlling large segments of the Nile Valley.

This victory opened a route southward and westward, isolating Alexandria from direct overland support.

15.4.3. Siege of Babylon Fortress and the Fall of Memphis

Near the old city of **Memphis** stood the fortress of **Babylon**, a strategic stronghold guarding the Nile crossing. Accounts vary, but a prolonged siege ensued:

- **Negotiations**: Some local leaders might have brokered deals to reduce bloodshed, while the garrison tried to hold out for reinforcements from Constantinople.
- **Surrender of Babylon**: Eventually, faced with diminishing hopes, the fortress surrendered. Arab forces thus controlled the heartland of Egypt, ensuring a steady flow of resources and intelligence.

15.4.4. Alexandria's Defense and Final Fall

The greatest challenge was capturing **Alexandria**, the seat of Byzantine administration:

1. **Byzantine Determination**: Emperor **Heraclius** had died in 641 CE, leaving a chaotic imperial succession. Nonetheless, the local Byzantine commander and Greek population resisted fiercely, leveraging city walls and naval connections.
2. **Naval Supremacy**: The Byzantines still controlled the sea, allowing some supplies to enter. But the Arab army cut off land routes, wore down the defenders, and negotiated with influential Alexandrians who saw no viable path to relief.
3. **Surrender (642 CE)**: After months of siege, Alexandria capitulated. A short-lived Byzantine recapture in 645–646 CE was reversed by the Arabs, sealing the fate of the province.

With Alexandria lost, Byzantine rule in Egypt came to an end. 'Amr ibn al-'As then made peace treaties with local communities, securing Arab governance over a region that had been under foreign dominion for nearly a millennium.

15.5. Establishing the New Administration

15.5.1. Governance and Taxation

The conquering forces had to incorporate Egypt into the expanding caliphate. Key policies:

- **Jizya and Kharaj**: Non-Muslim populations paid a poll tax (**jizya**) and land tax (**kharaj**). In return, their persons and property were protected, and they could continue practicing their religion.
- **Local Officials**: Egyptian scribes and administrators, many of whom were Copts, retained roles in record-keeping and tax collection. Their literacy and knowledge of the land made them indispensable.
- **Capital Shift**: Instead of adopting Alexandria as the capital, 'Amr founded a new garrison city called **Fustat** near the old fortress of Babylon (modern-day Cairo area). This separate city minimized friction between occupying troops and Alexandrian elites.

15.5.2. Religious Policy

The caliphate's approach to Christian communities was shaped by the principle of **dhimma**, a contract granting protected status to "People of the Book" (Christians, Jews) in exchange for taxes and acknowledgment of Muslim political authority.

- **Autonomy for the Coptic Church**: Local patriarchs and bishops oversaw religious matters. The new rulers typically refrained from interfering in doctrinal disputes—indeed, many Copts viewed Muslim governance as preferable to Chalcedonian persecution.
- **Gradual Conversion**: While many Egyptians remained Christian, some individuals converted to Islam, often to secure social or economic advantages (like reduced taxes). Over generations, the Muslim population expanded, but the shift was neither immediate nor forced by the state in this early period.

15.5.3. Arab Settlements

Arab soldiers and administrators established permanent settlements:

- **Fustat (al-Fustat)**: The first Islamic capital in Egypt, founded by 'Amr ibn al-'As. It included the mosque known as **Mosque of 'Amr ibn al-'As**, which became a religious and administrative center.
- **Garrisons Along the Nile**: Troops were stationed to deter any Byzantine attempt to retake the province.
- **Cultural Exchange**: Over time, intermarriage between Arab settlers and local Egyptians led to a blending of traditions, though Arabic only gradually supplanted Coptic as the dominant language.

15.6. Social and Economic Impact of the Conquest

15.6.1. Changes in Land Ownership

While some large estates remained under Greek or Coptic nobility, Arab officials introduced new forms of land grants to loyal military leaders. This process:

- **Continuity of Agriculture**: The Nile's irrigation cycle remained vital. Villagers still cultivated wheat, barley, vegetables, and flax. Tax structures changed, but the essential rural economy persisted.

- **Shift in Elite Status**: Greek landowners who cooperated with the new regime sometimes kept privileges, but many others lost influence to an emerging Arab-Muslim elite.

15.6.2. Trade and Commerce

Egypt's integration into the caliphate had significant commercial effects:

- **Mediterranean and Red Sea Networks**: Egyptian merchants tapped into expanding Islamic trade routes, linking North Africa, Arabia, and eventually the Indian Ocean.
- **Alexandria's Role**: Though no longer the capital, Alexandria remained an important maritime hub, facilitating the export of grain, papyrus, and textiles.
- **Urban Growth**: Fustat became a busy market city, attracting artisans, traders, and administrators. Over centuries, this settlement area merged with later Islamic capitals (al-Qata'i', al-Askar, and eventually Cairo).

15.6.3. Taxation Burdens

Initially, taxes rose for non-Muslims because of the **jizya** poll tax. However, the overall structure was a continuation of Byzantine practices: the land tax was a major source of revenue. Many peasants faced continued fiscal pressure, though they occasionally found the new regime more lenient than the previous one, especially regarding religious freedoms. Over time, shifting religious demographics—through conversions—affected state revenue strategies.

15.7. Religious Coexistence and Gradual Islamization

15.7.1. The Coptic Community Under Muslim Rule

The treaty terms negotiated by 'Amr ibn al-'As offered a degree of stability. Christian worship continued, and the Coptic Church handled internal matters such as marriage, inheritance, and clergy appointments. Sporadic unrest did occur:

- **Local Revolts**: Some uprisings flared, particularly if taxes were perceived as excessive. Yet these were usually localized events, subdued by quick military action.

- **No Forced Conversions**: In the early Rashidun and Umayyad periods, there was no widespread policy to force conversion. Copts who converted did so for social or economic reasons. Many continued their faith, retaining a Coptic patriarch in Alexandria.

15.7.2. Language and Identity

Over generations:

- **Arabic Administration**: The caliphate began introducing Arabic in official documents. By the 8th century, Arabic had replaced Greek and Coptic in government bureaus, spurring many Egyptians to learn the new language for social mobility.
- **Coptic Language Survival**: Coptic persisted in church liturgy and everyday conversation among rural communities. Over time, though, the prevalence of Arabic grew, shaping a new Egyptian identity blending Arab-Islamic and local traditions.

15.8. Consolidation Under the Umayyads and Abbasids

Although this chapter centers on the initial conquest, it is important to note the subsequent transitions:

15.8.1. Umayyad Rule (661–750 CE)

After the Rashidun period, the **Umayyad Caliphate** took power in Damascus. Their provincial governors in Egypt:

- **Enforced Arabic Administration**: They promoted the use of Arabic, minted coins, and reorganized fiscal systems.
- **Army Garrison**: Fustat remained the military headquarters. The city grew in influence, overshadowing older urban centers except for Alexandria's port.
- **Rebellions and Sectarian Divisions**: Some local disputes, including those involving the Kharijites or pro-Alid factions, periodically disturbed the region, but the Umayyads effectively controlled Egypt's grain exports, ensuring economic stability for the caliphate

15.8.2. Abbasid Dynasty (750–868 CE)

The **Abbasid Revolution** in 750 CE overthrew the Umayyads. Egypt became part of an empire ruled from Baghdad. Changes under the Abbasids:

- **Governors' Autonomy**: Abbasid caliphs appointed governors to manage Egypt, but distance from Baghdad allowed some governors significant autonomy.
- **Continuing Cultural Assimilation**: Arabic language and Islamic practices became even more entrenched among the population, though the Coptic Church remained a significant minority institution.
- **Economic Core**: Egypt continued as a crucial source of revenue and grain, bridging African and Middle Eastern trade routes.

All of these developments trace back to the initial conquest in the mid-7th century, which laid the groundwork for centuries of Islamic rule in Egypt.

15.9. The Significance of the Arab Conquest

15.9.1. A Turning Point in Egyptian History

Before the Arab conquest, Egypt had experienced multiple foreign dominations—Persian, Greek, Roman, and Byzantine—but each overlord largely preserved the older structures of a Hellenized or Romanized elite. By contrast, the Arab rulers introduced a **new religious framework** (Islam) and gradually **shifted the linguistic and cultural identity** of the region.

15.9.2. Enduring Legacy

- **Administrative Evolution**: From the founding of Fustat to the wide use of Arabic in bureaucracy, governance structures evolved in ways that still shape modern Egyptian administration.
- **Religious Dynamism**: Over the next centuries, Egypt transformed from a primarily Christian land into one with a Muslim majority. The Coptic Church survived but as a minority faith, preserving ancient Christian traditions.
- **Foundations for Later Dynasties**: The political machinery established by the early Arab governors set patterns for the Tulunids, Ikhshidids, Fatimids, and beyond, as each subsequent dynasty built upon the system of taxes, land grants, and centralized authority.

CHAPTER 16

THE FATIMID ERA

16.1. Introduction to the Fatimid Era (10th–12th Centuries CE)

The **Fatimid Dynasty** (909–1171 CE) represents a landmark in Egypt's medieval Islamic history. Initially arising in **Ifriqiya** (modern Tunisia) in **909 CE**, the Fatimids claimed descent from the Prophet's daughter **Fatima**, and followed the **Isma'ili** branch of Shi'a Islam. By the mid-10th century, Fatimid rulers turned their ambitions eastward, conquering **Egypt** in **969 CE** and establishing a new capital, **al-Qahira** (Cairo).

Under the Fatimids, Egypt evolved into a dynamic center of trade, learning, and religious discourse. The caliphs commissioned grand mosques, universities, and palaces, fostering the **Cairo** that would later become a major metropolis of the Islamic world. The Fatimids extended their influence across North Africa, the Levant, and even parts of the Red Sea coast, although they faced challenges from rivals like the Abbasids, local Sunni dynasties, and eventually the Crusaders.

This chapter explores the Fatimid rise to power, their conquest of Egypt, the policies that shaped their caliphate, the flourishing of arts and scholarship, and the eventual decline that paved the way for the **Ayyubid** period. By examining Fatimid rule, we see how Egypt functioned as a political and cultural crossroads during a vibrant yet turbulent phase of Islamic history.

16.2. Early Fatimid Background in North Africa

16.2.1. Isma'ili Shi'ism and the Mahdi

The Fatimid movement began with secretive **Isma'ili missionary** activities across the Islamic world, notably in North Africa. They recognized an unbroken line of imams descending from Isma'il, a son of the sixth Shi'a imam, Ja'far al-Sadiq. According to Isma'ili belief:

- **Hidden Imam**: The true imam was in occultation, soon to appear as the **Mahdi** (a messianic figure) who would restore justice.

- **'Ubayd Allah al-Mahdi**: Claimed to be this awaited imam. He emerged in Ifriqiya under the protection of local Berber tribes who supported his spiritual and political claims. In **909 CE**, he declared himself caliph, challenging the Sunni Abbasids in Baghdad.

16.2.2. Founding the Fatimid State in Ifriqiya

From their base in **Qayrawan** and later the newly founded capital of **Mahdia** on the Tunisian coast, the Fatimids built a strong power structure:

- **Berber Allies**: Tribes like the Kutama formed the backbone of their army.
- **Economic Stability**: Control of fertile farmland and Mediterranean trade routes financed the administration.
- **Conflict with the Abbasids**: Occasional naval skirmishes and land campaigns in Sicily, Sardinia, and mainland North Africa. The Fatimids positioned themselves as the legitimate caliphs in opposition to the Abbasids.

However, the limited resources of Ifriqiya motivated the Fatimids to seek the wealthier lands of Egypt and the Levant, culminating in a major campaign eastward.

16.3. The Conquest of Egypt (969 CE)

16.3.1. Decline of the Ikhshidids and the Path for Fatimid Advance

Before the Fatimids, Egypt was governed by the **Ikhshidid** dynasty (935–969 CE), nominally under the Abbasid Caliphate. Factors that weakened the Ikhshidids included:

- **Deaths of Key Rulers**: The founder, Muhammad ibn Tughj al-Ikhshid, and his capable successor both died, leaving child heirs and regents who struggled against internal factions.
- **Financial Instability**: Tax revenues diminished due to mismanagement and local revolts.
- **Military Challenges**: Rival dynasties and nomadic groups threatened the southern and western frontiers.

Sensing this vulnerability, the Fatimid caliph **al-Mu'izz li-Din Allah** launched a well-prepared campaign under the command of **Jawhar al-Siqilli** (Jawhar the Sicilian).

16.3.2. Jawhar's Campaign

In **969 CE**, Fatimid forces crossed into Egypt. The Ikhshidid governor, aware of the formidable Fatimid army and lacking support from the Abbasids, negotiated rather than fought a protracted war.

- **Peaceful Surrender of Fustat**: Jawhar promised security and religious tolerance for Sunni Muslims, Christians, and Jews if they accepted Fatimid rule.
- **Treaty of Fustat**: Freed the Egyptian population from pillage or heavy reprisals, in exchange for loyalty and regular tribute. This policy minimized resistance and secured a smooth transition of power.

By **July 969 CE**, Egypt was firmly under Fatimid control, marking a shift from Sunni Abbasid dominance to an Isma'ili Shi'a caliphate headquartered in the Nile Valley.

16.3.3. Founding of al-Qahira (Cairo)

Jawhar immediately began constructing a new palace-city north of Fustat. Known as **al-Mansuriyya** at first, it was soon renamed **al-Qahira** (Cairo), meaning "the victorious." Key features:

- **Royal Enclosure**: Fortified walls enclosed palaces, administrative offices, and the al-Azhar mosque.
- **Strategic Layout**: Distinct from older cities (Fustat, al-'Askar, al-Qata'i'), Cairo served as a ceremonial and political hub for the Fatimid court.
- **Mosque of al-Azhar**: Founded in 970 CE, it became a center of Isma'ili teaching and eventually one of the oldest universities in the Islamic world.

16.4. Fatimid Governance and Administration

16.4.1. Caliphal Authority and Isma'ili Shi'a Identity

The Fatimid caliph held both spiritual and temporal power. As an Isma'ili imam, he was revered by followers who believed he possessed divine guidance. This dual status shaped governance:

- **Spiritual Legitimacy**: The caliph's proclamations carried the weight of religious authority.
- **Council of Viziers**: The caliph's viziers handled daily administration, finances, and military affairs. Some viziers, like **Badr al-Jamali** and **al-Afdal**, wielded great influence, especially during weaker caliphs' reigns.

Although the Fatimids championed Isma'ili Shi'ism, they generally adopted a policy of tolerance toward the majority Sunni population, as well as Christian and Jewish communities, as long as they recognized Fatimid sovereignty.

16.4.2. Taxation and Land Policy

Egypt's fertility and strategic trade position provided the Fatimids with ample revenue:

- **Land Tax (Kharaj)**: Continued from earlier Islamic and even pre-Islamic systems. Peasants supplied grain and cash to provincial administrators.
- **Customs Duties**: Cairo's position on the spice and gold routes led to profitable tariffs on imported goods from the Red Sea and Indian Ocean.
- **Agricultural Projects**: Canals and irrigation works were maintained or improved. When the Nile floods were favorable, surpluses financed grand architectural ventures and the caliph's court.

16.4.3. Military Organization

Fatimid armies consisted of:

- **Berber Units**: Loyal contingents from the founding days in Ifriqiya.
- **Turkish and Sudanese Regiments**: Hired or enslaved soldiers (mamluks) added professional skill and manpower.
- **Naval Fleet**: Based in Alexandria, crucial for controlling maritime trade and repelling Byzantine or other naval threats.

Commanders were rotated to prevent any single ethnic group from dominating, though internal rivalries sometimes destabilized the court.

16.5. Cultural Flourishing Under the Fatimids

16.5.1. Architecture and Urban Development

Fatimid monuments in Cairo and beyond reflect a distinctive style:

1. **Mosque of al-Azhar**: Initially small, it underwent multiple expansions. It became a focal point of learning—today recognized as al-Azhar University.
2. **Mosque of al-Hakim**: Commissioned by Caliph al-Hakim bi-Amr Allah (996–1021 CE). Known for its massive minarets and austere grandeur, exemplifying Fatimid architectural innovation.
3. **City Walls and Gates**: Under **Badr al-Jamali** in the late 11th century, strong fortifications were built around Cairo. Gates like **Bab al-Futuh**, **Bab al-Nasr**, and **Bab Zuweila** remain landmarks, showcasing masterful stonework.

16.5.2. Arts, Crafts, and Luxury Goods

Fatimid society valued craftsmanship, with a courtly culture that prized luxury items:

- **Textiles**: Fine linens and silks, often adorned with calligraphic bands or figural motifs, were produced in royal workshops.
- **Ceramics and Glass**: Lustre-painted pottery and enameled glass from Fatimid ateliers were exported across the Mediterranean.
- **Metalwork and Jewelry**: Artisans created intricate inlaid bronze lamps, caskets, and gold or silver ornaments reflecting geometric and floral designs.

Such arts not only served local elites but also fueled trade networks with Europe and the Middle East.

16.5.3. Intellectual and Religious Life

The Fatimids encouraged scholarship in various fields:

- **Isma'ili Mission (Da'wa)**: Missionaries and scholars spread Fatimid doctrines abroad, debating theology with Sunni and Twelver Shi'a rivals.

- **Libraries and Academies**: Caliphs like al-Hakim and al-Mustanṣir maintained libraries containing volumes on philosophy, astronomy, medicine, and law.
- **Science and Philosophy**: While overshadowed by Baghdad's academic heritage, Cairo cultivated mathematicians, physicians, and philosophers, some of whom engaged in lively discourse with Jewish and Christian scholars in the city.

This environment fostered cross-cultural intellectual exchanges, making Fatimid Cairo a cosmopolitan hub.

16.6. Relations with Neighboring Powers

16.6.1. Conflict with the Abbasids

The Fatimids posed a direct ideological challenge to the **Sunni Abbasid Caliphate** in Baghdad. Over centuries:

- **Proxy Battles**: Both sides used provincial governors or local dynasties as proxies. In Syria, for example, the Fatimids vied with Abbasid-affiliated powers for control.
- **Sectarian Tensions**: Sunni rulers in the East denounced Fatimids as heretics, but practical alliances sometimes formed when common interests aligned, such as opposing Byzantium.

16.6.2. Interaction with the Byzantine Empire

Although Byzantium had lost Egypt in the 7th century, it remained a regional force:

- **Trade and Diplomatic Exchanges**: The Mediterranean commerce included Byzantine merchants in Alexandria. Occasionally, treaties regulated shipping and prisoner exchanges.
- **Naval Skirmishes**: Disputes flared over the Levantine coast or coastal raids, but neither side could force a decisive outcome given the distances involved.

16.6.3. The Crusades (Late 11th–12th Centuries)

When Latin Crusaders captured Jerusalem in **1099 CE**, the Fatimids had controlled the city just prior to that conquest. Egypt faced a new threat:

- **Battle of Ascalon (1099)**: The Crusaders defeated a Fatimid army near Ascalon, solidifying the Crusader presence in the Levant.
- **Balance of Power**: The Fatimids struggled to reclaim Palestine, while Crusaders never fully penetrated Egypt. This stalemate shaped regional politics until later Muslim leaders, like **Saladin** (who served as a Fatimid vizier before founding the Ayyubid dynasty), contested the Crusader states more effectively.

16.7. Internal Struggles and Decline of the Fatimids

16.7.1. Succession Disputes and Vizier Power

As the dynasty progressed, weak or young caliphs became puppets of powerful viziers:

- **al-Hakim's Mysterious Disappearance**: In 1021, al-Hakim vanished during a nighttime walk on the Muqattam hills. Rumors abounded—some Isma'ili sects even considered him divine, while mainstream Fatimids continued the caliphate under his successors.
- **Dynastic Feuds**: Intrigues among court officials and caliphal relatives destabilized the realm.
- **Vizier Dominance**: Viziers like **Badr al-Jamali** (1074–1094) and **al-Afdal** (1094–1121) revived Fatimid fortunes for a time. Yet, overreliance on a single strong minister caused abrupt shifts when that minister died or was deposed.

16.7.2. Economic Hardships

Egypt's prosperity depended heavily on the **Nile's** consistent floods. Periodic low floods led to famines, the worst occurring under al-Mustansir (1036–1094) in the mid-11th century:

- **Severe Famine (1050s–1060s)**: Known as the "Long Crisis" or "Great Famine," it caused widespread starvation, depopulation, and social unrest.

- **Loss of Control**: Rebellions in Upper Egypt and Syria further drained resources.
- **Reform Attempts**: Viziers attempted to reorganize the tax system and quell banditry, but repeated natural and political disasters eroded stability.

16.7.3. Rise of Sunni Sentiment and External Threats

Because the Fatimids followed Isma'ili Shi'ism, many of their Sunni subjects never fully embraced the caliphs' spiritual claims. This discontent, combined with pressure from the Sunni Abbasid-led world, steadily undermined Fatimid authority. By the 12th century, the caliphate's foreign policy failures and internal fracturing invited ambitious leaders to step in.

16.8. The Final Phase and the Transition to Ayyubid Rule

16.8.1. Saladin's Emergence

A pivotal figure in the Fatimid collapse was **Salah ad-Din** (Saladin), a Kurdish officer from the service of the Zengids in Syria. He entered Egypt as part of an expedition to support the Fatimids against Crusader and local threats:

- **Vizier to the Last Fatimid Caliphs**: Saladin took control of Cairo's government in 1169, nominally serving the young Fatimid caliph.
- **Restoration of Sunni Abbasid Authority**: Saladin quietly replaced Isma'ili judges with Sunni ones, curtailed the Fatimid da'wa, and built alliances with local Sunni groups.
- **Abolishing the Caliphate (1171)**: Upon the last Fatimid caliph's death, Saladin declared allegiance to the Abbasid Caliph in Baghdad, ending the Fatimid regime. He founded the **Ayyubid Dynasty** (1171–1250) that would shift Egypt firmly back into the Sunni fold.

16.8.2. Legacy of the Fatimids

Despite their final downfall:

- **Cairo's Enduring Importance**: The city they founded remained the political, cultural, and economic heart of Egypt.

- **Isma'ili Communities**: Some Isma'ili groups persisted in Egypt and the broader Islamic world. The **Dawoodi Bohras**, **Nizari Isma'ilis**, and other sects trace aspects of their religious heritage to Fatimid doctrines.
- **Architecture and Institutions**: Al-Azhar Mosque, city gates, and cultural tastes in jewelry and textiles reflect a Fatimid legacy still admired by historians and art connoisseurs.

16.9. Daily Life Under the Fatimids

16.9.1. Urban Society

Cairo became the seat of government, while Fustat thrived as a commercial hub:

- **Social Classes**: The caliph, royal family, and high officials sat atop the hierarchy, followed by military commanders, traders, and skilled artisans. Peasants and laborers formed the majority, taxed for the state's upkeep.
- **Markets and Souks**: Bazaars sold goods from across Africa, Europe, and Asia. Spices from India, gold from Nubia, and silks from Byzantium passed through Egyptian merchant networks.
- **Interfaith Interactions**: Christians and Jews lived in designated quarters, paying special taxes but often thriving as financiers or artisans. Cairo's "**Fustat Geniza**" documents reveal a cosmopolitan society exchanging letters, contracts, and religious texts in Hebrew, Arabic, and Judeo-Arabic.

16.9.2. Rural Realities

While Cairo's palaces gleamed with luxury:

- **Villagers**: Tilled fields, tended livestock, and endured occasional floods or droughts. The cycle of the Nile determined crop yields and tax burdens.
- **Coptic Communities**: In many rural areas, the population remained Christian, retaining their Coptic language for liturgy and local dealings. They supplied the caliphate with grains, vegetables, and possibly forced labor for canal maintenance.
- **Local Administration**: Appointed officials (often called 'amils) supervised villages, collecting taxes and overseeing minor disputes.

CHAPTER 17

THE AYYUBID AND MAMLUK PERIODS

17.1. Introduction

Following the **Fatimid Era** (969–1171 CE), Egypt entered a new phase of Islamic governance under the **Ayyubids** (1171–1250), led by the famous figure **Salah ad-Din** (Saladin). Afterward, the **Mamluks** (1250–1517) rose to power, creating a formidable sultanate renowned for its military might and architectural heritage. Together, these two periods spanned roughly four centuries and exerted profound influences on Egypt's religion, economy, and cultural identity.

During the Ayyubid era, Egypt saw a reassertion of **Sunni Islam** after decades of Isma'ili Shi'a rule under the Fatimids. Under Saladin and his successors, Cairo blossomed into a political and military capital, launching campaigns in Syria-Palestine against the Crusader states. The Mamluks, originally enslaved soldiers purchased by Ayyubid rulers, eventually seized power themselves, building a sultanate that defended the region from Mongol invasions and clashed with Crusaders. They sponsored lavish architectural projects in Cairo, leaving behind mosques, madrasas, and fortifications that still define the city's skyline.

In this chapter, we trace how Saladin consolidated power, how the Mamluks emerged from within Ayyubid structures to forge their own regime, and how these governments shaped Egypt's social, economic, and cultural trajectory. By the early 16th century, the Mamluk sultanate would fall to the advancing Ottoman Empire, ending this unique era of governance and setting the stage for the next chapter on the **Ottoman Period**.

17.2. The Ayyubid Dynasty (1171–1250)

17.2.1. Saladin's Rise to Power

Saladin (in Arabic, Salah ad-Din Yusuf ibn Ayyub) came from a Kurdish family in the service of the Zengid rulers of Syria. He arrived in **Fatimid Egypt** in 1169 as a lieutenant of the Zengid lord Nur ad-Din, officially to aid the weakening Fatimid regime against Crusaders and local rebels. However, Saladin soon became vizier to the last Fatimid caliph:

- **Dismantling the Fatimid Caliphate**: Saladin, a staunch Sunni, quietly replaced Isma'ili officials and ended the Fatimid caliphate upon the last caliph's death in 1171. He proclaimed allegiance to the **Abbasid Caliph** in Baghdad, re-establishing Sunni orthodoxy in Egypt.

- **Consolidation of Power**: After Nur ad-Din's death in 1174, Saladin declared independence, extending his control over Syria and parts of the Jazira region. Egypt became the core of his power base, supplying wealth and troops for his broader campaigns.

17.2.2. Ayyubid Governance in Egypt

Saladin and his successors, often called the **Ayyubids**, set up a dynastic rule characterized by:

1. **Family Appointments**: Saladin assigned governorships to his relatives—brothers, nephews, and sons—in key provinces like Damascus, Aleppo, and Yemen, forging a network of Ayyubid principalities.
2. **Sunni Religious Revival**: The Ayyubids promoted the construction of **Sunni madrasas** to propagate Shafi'i and Maliki jurisprudence. Sufi orders also gained patronage, expanding mystical Islam.
3. **Administrative Continuity**: Many Fatimid structures, especially in finance and irrigation management, remained. Skilled Coptic scribes and administrators continued to serve in bureaus, ensuring stability during the transition.

17.2.3. The Crusader Confrontation

Saladin's fame rests largely on his campaigns against the Latin Crusader states in the Levant:

- **Capture of Jerusalem (1187)**: At the **Battle of Hattin**, Saladin's forces defeated the Crusader army, paving the way for retaking Jerusalem. This victory elevated his reputation in the Islamic world as a champion of jihad.
- **Third Crusade (1189–1192)**: European leaders, including King Richard the Lionheart, responded. Though fierce battles raged—especially the siege of Acre—Saladin managed to hold on to most of his conquests, concluding a truce that allowed Muslim control over Jerusalem but permitted Christian pilgrims to visit.

In Egypt, Saladin funded his Levantine campaigns through tribute and taxation. He also secured the loyalty of military units by granting them **iqta'** (land assignments) and other privileges. Upon his death in 1193, the realm was divided among family members, leading to internal power struggles but overall Ayyubid continuity for several decades.

17.3. Ayyubid Society and Economy

17.3.1. Military and Land Tenure

The iqta' system, though not invented by the Ayyubids, became more defined under their rule:

- **Iqta' Grants**: Military officers received rights to collect taxes from specific regions or villages, in return for providing troops for the sultan. This arrangement tied the army's welfare to agricultural productivity, encouraging stable governance of rural areas.
- **Professional Soldiers**: Alongside Kurdish and Turkic contingents, the Ayyubids also employed **Mamluks**—enslaved soldiers purchased as children or adolescents and trained in warfare. Though initially loyal servants, these Mamluks would later challenge Ayyubid supremacy.

17.3.2. Trade and Urban Life

Egypt's economic prosperity under the Ayyubids came from:

1. **Agriculture**: As always, the Nile's floods guaranteed abundant harvests of grain and flax, taxed by the treasury.
2. **International Commerce**: Cairo-Fustat dominated East-West trade routes, funneling spices, metals, and textiles between India, the Middle East, and the Mediterranean.
3. **Urban Growth**: Cairo expanded beyond the old Fatimid walls, with new districts housing artisans, merchants, and religious institutions. The city's population included Muslims (Arab, Kurdish, Turkic), native Copts, and small Jewish and Christian foreign merchant communities.

17.3.3. Religious Policy

While staunchly Sunni, the Ayyubids generally showed tolerance toward Christians and Jews, who played key roles in commerce and administration. However:

- **Isma'ili Communities**: After dismantling the Fatimid da'wa, Isma'ili groups were sidelined. Some converted or practiced discreetly.
- **Patronage of Sunni Learning**: Saladin's building of madrasas—for example, the **Madrasa of Salih Najm ad-Din Ayyub**—signaled a new era of Sunni orthodoxy, further erasing the Fatimid Shi'a legacy in public life.

Despite these sectarian shifts, the Ayyubids avoided large-scale persecution, focusing on unity in the face of Crusader threats.

17.4. Decline of the Ayyubids and Rise of the Mamluks

17.4.1. Ayyubid Fragmentation

After Saladin's death, the Ayyubid dominion splintered:

- **Multiple Branches**: Saladin's relatives ruled in Damascus, Aleppo, Hama, Yemen, and Egypt, often competing for supremacy.
- **Egyptian Sultanate**: By the early 13th century, the Egyptian branch emerged dominant, but internal feuds and external pressures persisted.
- **Threats from Crusaders**: The Fifth Crusade (1217–1221) targeted Egypt, temporarily capturing Damietta on the Nile Delta. Al-Kamil, the Ayyubid sultan, eventually negotiated to expel the Crusaders, but these conflicts drained resources.

17.4.2. Al-Salih Ayyub and the Mamluks' Emergence

The final strong Ayyubid ruler in Egypt was **as-Salih Ayyub** (r. 1240–1249):

- **Dependence on Mamluks**: As-Salih Ayyub built a powerful corps of Mamluk soldiers, loyal to him personally. This corps was quartered on **Rawda Island** in Cairo.
- **Seventh Crusade (1248–1254)**: Led by King Louis IX of France, this campaign again targeted Damietta. As-Salih Ayyub died mid-campaign, leaving Egypt in a precarious position.

- **Victory at Mansurah (1250)**: The Mamluk generals, including **Baybars** and **Qutuz**, coordinated to defeat Louis IX's forces. Their success gave the Mamluks immense prestige. Soon, as-Salih's widow, **Shajar al-Durr**, and the Mamluk officers orchestrated the fall of the last Ayyubid heirs in Egypt, seizing power for themselves.

In **1250 CE**, the Mamluks formally ended Ayyubid rule, proclaiming their own sultanate. This shift, though sudden, had long roots in the Mamluks' central military role under the late Ayyubids.

17.5. The Mamluk Sultanate (1250–1517)

17.5.1. Founding and Early Challenges

The Mamluk sultanate is often divided into two phases:

1. **Bahri Mamluks (1250–1382)**: Named after the Bahriyya regiment stationed on Rawda Island in the Nile.
2. **Burji Mamluks (1382–1517)**: Originating from a different Mamluk faction centered at the Citadel of Cairo.

From the start, Mamluk rule faced internal power struggles and external threats—most notably from the **Mongols** and the Crusaders.

17.5.2. Social Foundations of Mamluk Power

Mamluks were originally enslaved youths, purchased from the steppes of Central Asia or the Caucasus. They converted to Islam and trained as elite cavalry. Upon emancipation, many rose to high ranks:

- **Military Meritocracy**: Unlike hereditary monarchies, Mamluk authority depended on martial prowess, loyalty, and skill in politics.
- **Alliance Building**: Successful sultans forged coalitions with senior Mamluk officers, religious scholars, and urban notables, balancing competing factions.
- **Patron-Client Ties**: Each Mamluk "household" or faction often supported a succession of sultans from within its ranks, leading to frequent palace coups.

17.5.3. Defense Against Mongols and Crusaders

The Mamluks are famed for repelling two formidable foes:

1. **Mongols**: In **1260**, the Mamluk sultan Qutuz (with notable general Baybars) defeated the Mongols at the **Battle of 'Ain Jalut** in Palestine—one of history's turning points halting Mongol expansion westward.
2. **Crusaders**: After consolidating power, sultans like **Baybars (r. 1260–1277)** and **Qalawun** launched campaigns to expel remaining Crusader enclaves in the Levant. By 1291, the last major Crusader stronghold at Acre fell, effectively ending Latin rule in the Holy Land.

These victories made the Mamluks the defenders of the Islamic Middle East, enhancing their legitimacy at home and abroad.

17.6. Mamluk Administration and Society

17.6.1. Military-Feudal Structures

Similar to Ayyubid iqta' allocations, Mamluk sultans granted military fiefs to officers:

- **Iqta' System**: Each Mamluk commander collected taxes from peasants in assigned districts, used to maintain troops and equipment.
- **Central Control**: The sultan's administrative council supervised these grants, ensuring no single amir (commander) became too powerful. Regular reassignments of iqta' lands prevented entrenched regional dynasties.

17.6.2. Legal and Religious Institutions

Mamluk sultans publicly embraced Sunni Islam, supporting the **four schools of law** (Hanafi, Maliki, Shafi'i, Hanbali) and patronizing religious scholars. Cairo's religious life flourished:

- **Madrasas**: Institutions to train jurists and theologians. Sultans founded numerous madrasas, endowing them with waqf (charitable trust) income.
- **Sufi Orders**: Various tariqas (Sufi brotherhoods) gained popularity. Mamluks often built khanqahs (Sufi lodges) to show piety and earn goodwill.

- **Judiciary**: Chief qadis for each law school managed courts. Copts and other non-Muslims had their own limited judicial autonomy for personal matters.

This synergy of military governance and religious patronage reinforced Mamluk legitimacy among Egypt's majority Muslim population.

17.6.3. Economy and Trade

Egypt's prosperity under Mamluk rule derived from:

1. **Agricultural Base**: Stable irrigation allowed high cereal production and taxes. The sultans invested in canal repairs, though corruption and local oppression sometimes undermined efficiency.
2. **Strategic Trade**: Cairo and Alexandria prospered as conduits for spices, precious metals, and other commodities from Asia to Europe. The Mamluks taxed commercial caravans and shipping lanes, funding lavish architectural projects.
3. **Monetary Policy**: The Mamluk dinar was widely recognized, though periodic currency debasement occurred. Economic fluctuations linked to plague epidemics (e.g., the Black Death in the mid-14th century) caused temporary dislocation.

Despite these complexities, the Mamluk era witnessed significant urban growth, especially in Cairo, which became a primary metropolis of the Islamic world.

17.7. Mamluk Culture and Architecture

17.7.1. Architectural Achievements

Mamluk sultans expressed power and piety through monumental construction, shaping Cairo's skyline with mosques, madrasas, mausoleums, and commercial complexes:

- **Sultan Hasan Mosque-Madrasa (14th century)**: A grand complex in Cairo, showcasing soaring minarets and elegant stonework. Considered one of the finest examples of Mamluk architecture.
- **Qalawun Complex (13th century)**: Combining a madrasa, hospital (maristan), and mausoleum near the old Fatimid heart of Cairo. Its ornate

decoration and use of marble panels reflect a unique blend of Islamic artistic traditions.
- **Minarets and Domes**: Mamluk structures often featured elaborate domes with carved geometric or floral patterns, plus tall, slender minarets distinguishing each sultan's building patronage.

17.7.2. Arts and Crafts

Patronage extended to the decorative arts:

1. **Metalwork**: Inlaid brass and bronze objects, such as lamps, candlesticks, and ewers, with inscriptions praising sultans or amirs.
2. **Glass and Enamel**: Mosque lamps were a signature product, adorned with enameled calligraphy and floral motifs.
3. **Manuscript Production**: Copyists and calligraphers in Cairo produced Qur'anic manuscripts of exquisite quality, often decorated with gold leaf and intricate margins.

17.7.3. Scholarship and Literature

While military pursuits dominated Mamluk life, intellectual culture also thrived:

- **Religious Scholarship**: Eminent jurists and theologians wrote commentaries on Islamic law and dogma.
- **Historiography**: Chroniclers like **Ibn Taghribirdi** and **al-Maqrizi** documented Mamluk events, city topography, and administrative systems, leaving rich sources for future historians.
- **Sufi Literature**: Mystical poetry and treatises flourished in Cairo's Sufi lodges, blending local traditions with influences from Syria, Iraq, and beyond.

This dynamic cultural scene showcased a blend of martial ethos and refined tastes, uniting diverse peoples under Mamluk rule.

17.8. Challenges and Decline of the Mamluks

17.8.1. Internal Strife and Overextension

Maintaining cohesion was a constant struggle:

- **Factional Coups**: Rival Mamluk factions at the court often vied for power, resulting in a rapid turnover of sultans. Some reigns lasted mere months before a palace conspiracy installed a new ruler.
- **Fiscal Instability**: Military campaigns and lavish spending on architecture strained the treasury. Over-farming and corruption in iqta' administration damaged agricultural productivity.

17.8.2. External Pressures

By the late 15th century, major changes loomed:

- **Shift in Global Trade Routes**: European exploration of sea routes to Asia reduced reliance on the Red Sea—overland routes shrank. Mamluk revenues from spice transit diminished, weakening the sultanate's economic base.
- **Ottoman Expansion**: The rising Ottoman Empire, controlling Anatolia and the Balkans, posed a significant threat. Diplomatic friction with the Mamluks worsened over claims to Syria and border territories.

17.8.3. The Ottoman Conquest (1516–1517)

Final blows came from the Ottoman sultans Selim I and Süleyman:

- **Battle of Marj Dabiq (1516)** in northern Syria: Ottoman forces routed the Mamluk army, opening the way to Damascus.
- **Battle of Ridaniya (1517)** near Cairo: Decisive Ottoman victory ended Mamluk independence. The last Mamluk sultan, Tuman Bay II, resisted but was eventually captured and executed.
- **Incorporation into the Ottoman Empire**: Egypt became an Ottoman province in 1517, though former Mamluks remained influential as local elites under Ottoman oversight.

Thus concluded nearly three centuries of Mamluk rule, which left a deep imprint on Egyptian governance, culture, and architecture.

17.9. Society Under the Ayyubid-Mamluk Transitions

Though overshadowed by high-level politics, everyday life for Egyptians during these eras combined continuity and adaptation:

- **Fellahin (Peasants)**: Their primary concern was cultivation, irrigation, and meeting tax obligations. Periodic revolts occurred when taxes became too burdensome.
- **Urban Artisans and Merchants**: Cairo's bazaars offered economic opportunities. Skilled artisans found patrons among amirs and sultans, while merchants profited from trade across Africa, Asia, and Europe.
- **Dhimmis (Christians and Jews)**: Largely tolerated, but faced occasional discriminatory regulations (clothing requirements, higher taxes). Still, many rose to respected positions as physicians, translators, or financiers.
- **Women's Roles**: Royal women, especially in the Mamluk court, sometimes influenced succession disputes or endowed charitable buildings. Elite families often lived in seclusion behind high walls, though ordinary women participated in market life, domestic tasks, and religious festivities.

Across these centuries, local Egyptians adapted to shifting dynastic powers. Agriculture remained the backbone, while cities like Cairo thrived as cultural melting pots. The Ayyubid restoration of Sunni Islam and the subsequent Mamluk emphasis on a strong military state both shaped Egypt's internal developments and external relations.

17.10. Conclusion of Chapter 17

The **Ayyubid and Mamluk Periods** (1171–1517) stand as a transformative epoch in Egypt's medieval history. **Saladin** ended Fatimid rule and reunited Egypt with the Sunni Muslim world, famously contesting the Crusader states and winning admiration throughout the Islamic sphere. His Ayyubid successors consolidated a dynastic system, but the reliance on Mamluk slave-soldiers set the stage for the next regime's emergence.

Seizing power in **1250**, the **Mamluks** protected the Middle East from Mongols and Crusaders, constructing a unique military elite that thrived on martial valor and elaborate cultural patronage. Their sultanate witnessed Cairo's rise as a grand metropolis, boasting monumental architecture and flourishing scholarship. Nonetheless, internal rivalries, economic strains, and the ascendancy of the Ottomans eventually toppled Mamluk rule in the early 16th century.

CHAPTER 18

THE OTTOMAN PERIOD

18.1. Introduction

With the **Ottoman conquest of Egypt** in **1517**, Egypt became an important province of the sprawling Ottoman Empire. Though no longer independent, the country retained considerable cultural and administrative distinctiveness. Ottoman governors oversaw Cairo, managing taxes, trade, and military affairs under the sultan's authority in Istanbul. However, local elites—including former Mamluks—remained influential, resulting in a complex power dynamic between the central Ottoman government and regional forces in Egypt.

Over the next three centuries, Egypt's fortunes rose and fell. Ottoman integration provided a vast imperial framework for commerce, yet changing global trade routes, internal mismanagement, and occasional rebellions hindered economic growth. By the late 18th century, external pressures—from European powers and local uprisings—would shake Ottoman control, paving the way for new regimes in the 19th century.

In this chapter, we explore how the Ottomans governed Egypt, how everyday life and social structures evolved, and how shifting geopolitical realities placed pressures on the province. We conclude by setting the stage for **Muhammad Ali** and his successors, who introduced a series of major reforms and ushered in a new chapter in Egyptian history.

18.2. The Ottoman Conquest and Establishment of Control

18.2.1. Selim I's Campaign (1516–1517)

The Ottoman sultan **Selim I** launched a decisive war against the Mamluks, defeating them at **Marj Dabiq** in 1516 (north of Aleppo) and at **Ridaniya** in 1517 (near Cairo). Major outcomes included:

- **Capture of Cairo**: The Ottomans deposed the last Mamluk sultan, Tuman Bay II, ending Mamluk sovereignty.

- **Incorporation into the Empire**: Egypt was placed under Ottoman rule, though some Mamluks negotiated to retain land and positions under Ottoman oversight.

18.2.2. Administrative Framework

Selim I appointed a **viceroy** or **governor** (called the **Wali** or **Pasha**) to represent Ottoman authority in Egypt. Key elements:

1. **Diwan (Council)**: A local council including top Ottoman officials, military commanders (janissary officers), and sometimes prominent Egyptian notables.
2. **Timar System**: Similar to the iqta', the Ottomans used the timar model, allotting land revenues to cavalry soldiers. However, in Egypt's case, direct taxation by the governor often overshadowed smaller timars.
3. **Residual Mamluk Influence**: Many Mamluk beys maintained control over provincial areas. Over time, they carved out autonomy, especially in the southern provinces, leading to a hybrid power structure.

Initially, the Ottomans dismantled Mamluk fortifications and confiscated wealth, but they soon realized they needed local elites to manage daily governance.

18.3. Governance and Power Struggles in Ottoman Egypt

18.3.1. The Role of the Governor (Pasha)

Ottoman sultans in Istanbul periodically replaced Egyptian governors to prevent local strongmen from entrenching themselves. Despite this, some governors wielded real authority, especially if they successfully balanced:

- **Military Backing**: A strong contingent of Ottoman soldiers (janissaries, spahis) stationed in the Cairo garrison.
- **Local Alliances**: Partnerships with influential Mamluk beys, tribal leaders, or urban notables could ensure stable taxation and security.
- **Compliance with Istanbul**: Regular tribute, stable order, and suppression of rebellions satisfied the Ottoman court.

18.3.2. Mamluk Revival as Provincial Power-Brokers

Surviving Mamluks adapted to Ottoman rule:

- **Beys and Households**: Mamluk beys, each with a retinue of retainers, became de facto provincial chiefs, collecting taxes and maintaining order in assigned districts.
- **Periodic Revolts**: Certain Mamluk factions occasionally challenged the Ottoman pasha, hoping to restore full autonomy. While not completely successful, these uprisings forced the Ottomans to negotiate.
- **Dual Authority**: Egyptian politics thus featured a delicate balance between the official Ottoman governor and powerful Mamluk warlords—each needing the other to manage the country effectively.

18.3.3. Janissaries and Local Garrison

The Ottoman Empire's elite infantry, the **janissaries**, manned Cairo's garrison, ensuring central control. Over time:

- **Integration**: Many janissaries married locally, establishing families and local commercial interests.
- **Factionalism**: Janissary corps sometimes split into rival groups, allying with or against Mamluk beys.
- **Mutinies**: When pay was delayed or conditions were poor, janissaries occasionally revolted, holding the governor hostage to their demands.

This interplay of Ottoman soldiers, Mamluk elites, and local leadership shaped Egyptian governance for centuries.

18.4. Economic Structures Under Ottoman Administration

18.4.1. Taxation and Revenue

The Ottomans relied heavily on Egyptian revenues:

1. **Fixed Tribute to Istanbul**: A set portion of Egypt's surplus, primarily in grain and cash, was shipped to the imperial center.
2. **Agricultural Taxes**: Peasants (fellahin) paid land taxes, often at high rates. Mamluk beys or appointed officials collected these taxes, retaining a share.

3. **Customs Duties**: Trade passing through Alexandria or Red Sea ports like Suez paid tariffs, supporting both local administration and the imperial treasury.

Frequent graft and corruption among tax collectors sometimes caused peasant unrest, but the Nile's fertility generally ensured a steady flow of resources.

18.4.2. International Trade

Egypt's position at the crossroads of Africa, the Middle East, and the Mediterranean continued to shape its commerce:

- **Shift in Global Routes**: Following Portuguese exploration of the Cape of Good Hope (late 15th century), direct sea routes to India bypassed the Red Sea. Egyptian revenues from the spice trade thus declined, though some Indian Ocean shipping still passed through Suez.
- **Caravan Trade**: Trans-Saharan routes brought gold, slaves, and ivory from sub-Saharan Africa. Egypt's merchants managed caravans linking Sudanese regions with Cairo.
- **European Interaction**: Venice, France, and other European powers maintained consulates in Alexandria or Rosetta, trading wool, timber, and metal goods for Egyptian grain, rice, and textiles.

While global competition reduced Egypt's previous monopoly on East-West spice trade, the country remained an important commercial hub in the Ottoman realm.

18.5. Social and Cultural Life in Ottoman Egypt

18.5.1. Religious Communities

Egypt under the Ottomans retained a pluralistic religious landscape:

- **Sunni Islam**: The dominant faith. The Hanafi school of jurisprudence was favored by Ottoman authorities, though local populations often followed Maliki or Shafi'i traditions.
- **Sufi Orders**: Confraternities like the Qadiriyya, Khalwatiyya, and Shadhiliyya thrived. Their zawiyas (lodges) provided spiritual guidance, charity, and community gatherings.

- **Coptic Christians**: Continued living under dhimma regulations, paying the jizya tax. Copts served as scribes, financiers, and in other administrative roles. Their patriarch in Alexandria maintained ecclesiastical authority.
- **Jewish Communities**: Centered mainly in Cairo and Alexandria, engaging in trade, banking, and crafts. They, too, experienced periodic restrictions or local tensions but generally coexisted under Ottoman laws protecting "People of the Book."

18.5.2. Urban Life in Cairo

Cairo remained Egypt's premier city:

1. **Neighborhoods and Quarters**: A patchwork of districts, each home to specific occupations or ethnic groups—e.g., the silversmith quarter, the Moroccan quarter, etc.
2. **Markets (Souks)**: Khan al-Khalili emerged as a famous commercial area, dealing in spices, textiles, and luxury goods.
3. **Religious Institutions**: Al-Azhar Mosque continued as a center of Islamic learning. Ottoman pashas funded renovations, and Mamluk endowments still supported many madrasas.
4. **Public Infrastructure**: Water supply systems, public fountains (sabils), and caravanserais (wakalas) catered to local residents and visiting traders. However, upkeep depended on the competence and integrity of local officials.

Despite political uncertainties, Cairo's cultural vibrancy persisted, echoing the city's Mamluk heritage while adapting to Ottoman norms.

18.5.3. Rural Communities

Villages operated under local headmen who coordinated irrigation schedules, collected taxes for the pasha, and mediated disputes:

- **Irrigation Cycles**: Each year's Nile flood determined prosperity or hardship. Skilled farmers used centuries-old knowledge to manage water distribution.
- **Peasant Hardships**: Forced labor (corvée) for canal cleaning and construction weighed heavily on the fellahin. High taxation sometimes led to migration or banditry.

- **Landholding Patterns**: Mamluk beys or Ottoman officials controlled large estates, renting plots to peasants at rates that varied according to local custom and negotiation.

18.6. Key Transformations in the 17th–18th Centuries

18.6.1. Decentralization and Local Autonomy

As the Ottoman central government faced internal and external challenges, local elites in Egypt gained power:

- **Mamluk Beys as De Facto Rulers**: Influential families like the Qasimiya or Fiqariyya factions contended for the office of **shaykh al-balad** (chief of the country), effectively governing the rural districts.
- **Power Struggles**: Rival beys fought one another in Cairo's streets, each seeking to dominate the diwan and control taxes. The Ottoman pasha often stood as an arbitrator or an onlooker, depending on his capabilities.

18.6.2. Economic Fluctuations

World events impacted Egypt's economy:

1. **Rise of European Maritime Powers**: Dutch, English, and French shipping increased competition in the Mediterranean, diminishing Ottoman monopolies.
2. **Agricultural Trends**: Some local elites invested in commercial cash crops—e.g., cotton or sugar—exported to European markets. Yet unpredictable Nile floods and locust invasions frequently hampered yields.
3. **Plague and Epidemics**: Recurrent outbreaks of plague reduced population and labor availability, exacerbating revenue shortfalls.

18.6.3. Cultural Continuity and Renewal

Despite difficulties, Egypt's intellectual and religious life remained vibrant:

- **Religious Scholarship**: Al-Azhar produced renowned ulema (scholars) who wrote treatises on Islamic jurisprudence, theology, and grammar.
- **Sufi Networks**: Expanded philanthropic and social roles. Certain Sufi saints gained widespread veneration, bridging communal divides.

- **Art and Architecture**: Ottoman governors and Mamluk beys continued to build mosques, sabil-kuttabs (combining a public water fountain and Qur'anic school), and mansions with elaborate mashrabiya (wooden latticework) windows. This merging of Ottoman style with local Mamluk traditions defined a distinctive Cairene aesthetic.

18.7. Foreign Intrusions and the Late Ottoman Period in Egypt

18.7.1. French Expedition Under Napoleon (1798–1801)

Though it lies slightly beyond the strict medieval timeline, the French invasion by **Napoleon Bonaparte** in 1798 profoundly illustrated Egypt's vulnerability:

- **Defeat of Mamluk Forces**: At the **Battle of the Pyramids**, French troops displayed modern tactics and firepower that outclassed the cavalry-based Mamluk beys.
- **Temporary Occupation**: Napoleon's ambitions to establish a presence in the Middle East disrupted the Ottoman domain. British naval power and Ottoman alliances eventually forced French withdrawal in 1801.
- **Impact on Egypt**: The French campaign revealed the archaic state of the local military and administration. Scholars accompanying Napoleon documented Egypt's antiquities, sparking European interest in Egyptology.

While not directly covered in earlier chapters, this event signals the declining grip of Ottoman control and the potential for European interference, setting the stage for 19th-century transformations.

18.7.2. Rise of Muhammad Ali

In the aftermath of the French exit, Ottoman authorities struggled to restore stable governance. Amid power contests between Ottoman-appointed governors and local Mamluk factions, a new figure emerged: **Muhammad Ali**. An Albanian officer in the Ottoman service, he maneuvered to outwit both Mamluks and Ottoman officials, becoming the undisputed ruler of Egypt by **1805**. This watershed moment marks the end of our current chapter's focus, as Muhammad Ali's reign heralded the modern era of Egyptian reforms and an evolving relationship with Europe and the Middle East.

18.8. Society and Culture in Late Ottoman Egypt

Though overshadowed by looming modernization, daily life still reflected traditional patterns:

- **Guilds and Crafts**: Artisans in Cairo's guilds produced textiles, metal goods, leather products, and other handicrafts. They regulated prices, training, and quality.
- **Festivals and Religious Celebrations**: Mawlid (saints' birthdays) and other festivities brought together different classes, reinforcing community ties. The Nile flood festival remained a major occasion, marking life's dependence on the river's bounty.
- **Literacy and Education**: Limited to religious institutions, wealthy families sometimes hired private tutors. Al-Azhar served as the principal university, though overshadowed by newer educational ideals introduced in the 19th century.

Even as European powers cast a long shadow, Ottoman Egypt displayed resilience, preserving longstanding social frameworks in the face of global change.

18.9. Legacy of Ottoman Rule in Egypt

Despite periods of stagnation and local fragmentation, Ottoman rule had lasting effects on Egyptian history:

1. **Administrative Structures**: Provincial governance, reliance on local elites, and a layered approach to authority became entrenched features of Egyptian politics.
2. **Cultural Synthesis**: Ottoman architectural forms merged with lingering Mamluk styles in mosques, palaces, and civic buildings. The Turkish language influenced courtly culture, though Arabic remained dominant among the populace.
3. **Path to Modern Statehood**: The weaknesses exposed under Ottoman dominion set the stage for ambitious 19th-century leaders—like Muhammad Ali—who leveraged foreign alliances, reorganized the army, and reformed administration to carve a new path for Egypt.

CHAPTER 19

EGYPT UNDER MUHAMMAD ALI AND HIS SUCCESSORS

19.1. Introduction

By the early **19th century**, Egypt had been an **Ottoman province** for nearly three centuries. Internal strife between Ottoman-appointed governors, local Mamluk leaders, and factions in Cairo had weakened effective governance. Against this backdrop emerged an ambitious figure: **Muhammad Ali Pasha** (Mehmet Ali), an Albanian officer serving in the Ottoman army, who maneuvered to outwit both his Ottoman superiors and the powerful Mamluks. By **1805**, Muhammad Ali had secured the title of **Wali** (governor) of Egypt, gradually transforming the province into a de facto independent state under his personal rule.

This chapter explores the key reforms that Muhammad Ali introduced in the military, economy, and social arenas, setting Egypt on a path toward modernization—although still within a broader Ottoman framework. We will then examine the reigns of his successors, noting the extent to which they continued his policies or diverged. Throughout the 19th century, Egypt faced challenges from European powers, financial troubles, and internal changes, gradually ceding more influence to foreign creditors. We conclude by briefly mentioning the pivotal events leading up to the late 19th century, without venturing deeply into modern history.

19.2. Muhammad Ali's Rise to Power (1801–1805)

19.2.1. Aftermath of the French Occupation

When **Napoleon Bonaparte** invaded Egypt in **1798**, the Mamluk beys proved unable to mount an effective defense. The French occupation lasted until **1801**, when British and Ottoman forces forced the French withdrawal. Chaos reigned as various leaders tried to claim power:

- **Ottoman Reassertion**: The empire sent governors, but faced difficulties controlling local elites.

- **Mamluk Factions**: Rival beys vied for dominance in Cairo and rural districts.
- **Albanian Troops**: Soldiers from the Balkans—among them Muhammad Ali—remained in Egypt to help restore order.

19.2.2. Emergence of Muhammad Ali

Muhammad Ali demonstrated strategic acumen. He formed alliances with local notables, promised stability, and eventually displaced or co-opted rivals. Key steps in his ascent:

1. **Popularity in Cairo**: He distributed grain in times of shortage, currying favor with the urban population and religious scholars.
2. **Support of the Ulama**: Leading ulema (Islamic scholars) recognized that Muhammad Ali was more reliable than rival governors, endorsing him to the Ottoman sultan.
3. **Official Appointment (1805)**: The Ottoman sultan recognized Muhammad Ali as Wali of Egypt, believing he would remain loyal to Istanbul.

Though nominally an Ottoman appointee, Muhammad Ali pursued policies that made Egypt increasingly autonomous, forging a centralized state under his control.

19.3. Consolidating Authority: The Massacre of the Mamluks

19.3.1. Mamluk Power in Decline

Despite Ottoman conquests, many **Mamluks** had survived as provincial landholders. They still possessed local militias and extracted taxes, undermining Muhammad Ali's quest for absolute authority. He initially attempted negotiations, but tensions grew.

19.3.2. The Citadel Massacre (1811)

To eliminate the Mamluk threat, Muhammad Ali orchestrated a ruse:

- **Reception at the Citadel**: He invited leading Mamluk beys to celebrate the departure of an expeditionary force heading to Arabia.
- **Ambush**: As the Mamluks passed through a narrow gate within the Citadel, Muhammad Ali's troops ambushed them. Many Mamluk leaders

were killed on the spot; those who fled down the cliffs were pursued and eliminated.
- **Aftermath**: This event effectively shattered the Mamluk aristocracy in Cairo. Although some Mamluks survived in rural or distant areas, they no longer posed a unified challenge.

With the Mamluks curtailed, Muhammad Ali stood unopposed in Egyptian politics, free to institute broad reforms.

19.4. Military and Administrative Reforms

19.4.1. Building a Modern Army

Muhammad Ali recognized that a strong, modern army was essential for defending and expanding Egyptian interests. He introduced:

1. **Conscription**: Egyptian peasants (fellahin) were drafted, a drastic shift from the previous reliance on Mamluk cavalry or mercenaries. Many peasants resented conscription, viewing it as harsh and uprooting them from agricultural life.
2. **European Expertise**: Muhammad Ali hired European advisors—French, Italian, or others—who taught modern drill, artillery, and organizational methods.
3. **Arsenal and Factories**: He established weapons workshops near Cairo to produce muskets, cannons, and ammunition. Egypt thus reduced dependence on foreign arms suppliers.

These measures transformed the Egyptian military into a formidable force, enabling campaigns in Arabia, Sudan, and beyond.

19.4.2. Centralized Administration

To finance his new army and maintain control:

- **Land Nationalization**: Muhammad Ali took direct possession of most agricultural land, making the state effectively the sole landlord. Farmers were ordered to deliver produce to state agents at fixed prices, generating revenue for the treasury.

- **Bureaucratic Hierarchy**: He created ministries to oversee agriculture, trade, finance, and public works, staffed by loyal officials—often drawn from families trained in new schools.
- **Province Reorganization**: Governors and sub-governors were appointed to manage each region, reporting directly to Cairo. This system curtailed local autonomy.

These administrative moves placed unprecedented power in Muhammad Ali's hands, forging a more centralized state than any in Egypt since the Mamluk sultanate had collapsed under Ottoman rule.

19.5. Economic Initiatives and Industrial Experiments

19.5.1. Cash Crops and Monopolies

Keen on boosting treasury income:

1. **Cotton Cultivation**: Muhammad Ali promoted long-staple cotton in the Nile Delta, turning Egypt into a key raw cotton exporter. This decision would reshape rural economies and link Egypt closer to European textile industries—particularly in Britain.
2. **State Monopolies**: The government set prices and controlled trade for cotton, wheat, and other crops, consolidating profits. Merchants were compelled to sell at official depots.
3. **Infrastructure**: He improved irrigation canals, constructed dams, and began modernization projects at ports like Alexandria, all to streamline export flows.

19.5.2. Early Industrial Projects

Hoping to reduce reliance on foreign manufactures:

- **Textile Mills**: Factories near Cairo attempted to process Egyptian cotton into cloth.
- **Shipbuilding**: Shipyards in Alexandria tried producing warships and merchant vessels.
- **Challenges**: A lack of skilled labor, high costs, and limited domestic markets hindered many industrial ventures. Despite partial successes, most factories struggled to compete against established European industry.

Although these enterprises did not fully flourish, they revealed an ambitious vision of economic development rarely seen in other Ottoman provinces.

19.6. Educational and Social Reforms

19.6.1. New Schools and European Training Missions

Muhammad Ali recognized the importance of trained officials and technicians:

1. **Schools of Medicine, Engineering, and Administration**: Established in or near Cairo, taught by European instructors or by Egyptians who had studied abroad.
2. **Student Missions to Europe**: Groups of young Egyptians were sent to France or Italy to study modern sciences, returning to fill government posts.
3. **Language Shift**: Arabic began to blend with some European concepts in technical vocabularies, though Turkish remained the language of the elite court. Over time, bilingual officials emerged.

19.6.2. Social Consequences

Reforms mainly benefited a small circle of elites and educated youth:

- **Peasant Hardship**: High taxation, forced labor for public works, and harsh conscription practices weighed heavily on rural Egyptians.
- **Women's Status**: Reforms did little to alter traditional gender roles. Elite women sometimes experienced new influences (e.g., wearing European fashions at court), but broad societal norms stayed the same.
- **Urban Growth**: Cairo, Alexandria, and other towns expanded, housing new factories, schools, and administrative bureaus, giving rise to a modest middle stratum of merchants, civil servants, and professionals.

19.7. Foreign Campaigns and Diplomatic Strains

19.7.1. Military Expeditions in the Region

With his modernized army, Muhammad Ali embarked on campaigns to enhance his power:

1. **Wahhabi Campaign (1811–1818)**: At the Ottoman sultan's behest, he dispatched Egyptian forces to Arabia, suppressing the Wahhabi rebels in the Hijaz region.
2. **Sudan Conquests**: He extended Egyptian rule southward, hoping to gain gold, slaves, and new farmland. Egyptian forces established posts along the Nile in present-day Sudan.
3. **Greek War of Independence (1821–1829)**: At the sultan's request, Muhammad Ali intervened in Greece. His son Ibrahim Pasha led Egyptian troops, but European powers (Britain, France, Russia) supported Greek independence, ultimately forcing an Egyptian withdrawal.

19.7.2. Conflict with the Ottoman Sultan

Muhammad Ali's successes fueled his ambition, leading to open conflict with his nominal overlord, the Ottoman sultan:

- **Syrian Campaign (1831–1833)**: Under Ibrahim Pasha, Egyptian forces invaded Ottoman Syria. They defeated the sultan's troops, threatening Istanbul itself. European powers stepped in, compelling Muhammad Ali to return some territories but granting him hereditary rule over Egypt.
- **Renewed Tensions (1839–1841)**: Another Ottoman attempt to break Muhammad Ali's power ended with further European arbitration. A settlement confirmed that the governorship of Egypt would remain hereditary in Muhammad Ali's family, but forced him to reduce his military expansions.

These confrontations revealed the tensions between a resurgent Egypt and an Ottoman Empire struggling to modernize under external pressure. European intervention indicated a rising interest in the region, foreshadowing future foreign entanglements.

19.8. Succession and Later Khedives

19.8.1. Late Reign of Muhammad Ali

In his final years, Muhammad Ali's health declined:

- **Mental Fatigue**: By the mid-1840s, he suffered episodes of confusion, effectively ceding day-to-day rule to his son Ibrahim Pasha.

- **Death (1849)**: Muhammad Ali died as one of the Middle East's most notable rulers—celebrated for modernization, criticized for harsh methods and personal ambition.

19.8.2. Ibrahim Pasha and Abbas I

- **Ibrahim Pasha**: Briefly held power but died soon after his father. Under him, some reforms continued, although resources were stretched thin from military ventures.
- **Abbas I (r. 1848–1854)**: A more conservative figure, Abbas reversed certain state monopolies and closed some factories. He was suspicious of European advisors, halting some of his grandfather's modernization plans. He also allied closely with the Ottoman sultan, trying to reaffirm Egyptian loyalty.

19.8.3. Sa'id Pasha (r. 1854–1863)

Sa'id Pasha, another son of Muhammad Ali, reopened connections with Europe:

- **Legal and Fiscal Adjustments**: He reformed taxation, diminishing forced monopolies, and sought to calm peasants' grievances.
- **Suez Canal Concession**: Crucially, Sa'id granted a concession to French diplomat Ferdinand de Lesseps for constructing the Suez Canal. Although the canal project did not fully commence until Isma'il's reign, Sa'id's initial approval planted the seeds of a transformative infrastructure project that connected the Mediterranean to the Red Sea.

19.9. Isma'il Pasha and the Height of Ambition (r. 1863–1879)

19.9.1. Grand Projects and Modernizing Zeal

Isma'il Pasha, grandson of Muhammad Ali, ascended to power with grand visions:

1. **Infrastructure Boom**: Constructing railways, improving ports, digging new irrigation canals, and finishing the Suez Canal (opened in **1869**).
2. **Urban Development**: Cairo underwent significant redesign, with boulevards inspired by Paris. Public lighting, theaters, and grand palaces symbolized Egypt's modernization.

3. **Education and Culture**: Isma'il expanded schools, fostered printing presses, and patronized cultural events like the Opera House in Cairo—famously marking the premiere of Verdi's "Aida" (though its exact performance date is debated).

Isma'il's ambition earned him the personal title **Khedive** (viceroy) from the Ottoman sultan. Under his reign, Egypt seemed poised to join the ranks of modernizing states.

19.9.2. Mounting Debt and European Oversight

However, grandiose projects required massive loans from European banks:

- **Borrowing Spree**: Financing the Suez Canal's completion, lavish ceremonies (like the canal inauguration), and infrastructure soared in cost.
- **Revenue Shortfalls**: Despite raising taxes, the treasury could not meet the skyrocketing interest on foreign debt.
- **Foreign Control**: Alarmed creditors—especially Britain and France—pushed for financial oversight. By the late 1870s, international commissions managed parts of Egypt's budget, reducing the Khedive's autonomy.

As debt spiraled, Isma'il lost the support of European powers. They compelled the Ottoman sultan to depose him, installing his son Tewfik in 1879. Thus ended an era of flamboyant modernization overshadowed by financial crisis.

19.10. Prelude to Further Foreign Intervention

Though we avoid delving deeply into modern times, a brief mention clarifies how the 19th century ended:

- **Khedive Tewfik (r. 1879–1892)** faced the **'Urabi Revolt** (1881–1882), a nationalist uprising by army officers opposed to foreign financial control.
- **British Occupation (1882)**: Fearing instability could threaten their route to India via the Suez Canal, Britain intervened militarily. Egypt thus fell under "veiled protectorate" status, with British advisors exerting significant influence.

This period transitions Egypt from Muhammad Ali's semi-independent monarchy within the Ottoman domain to an era of European-dominated governance. Such developments shaped the early 20th century and beyond, though that modern trajectory lies outside our primary historical focus.

19.11. Socioeconomic Changes Under Muhammad Ali's Dynasty

19.11.1. Impact on Rural Society

- **Monoculture**: The push for cotton production tied peasants to cash crops. During cotton's profitable years, some farmers benefited, but reliance on a single export commodity risked vulnerability to market fluctuations.
- **Forced Labor**: The corvée system, demanding peasants build canals or railways under harsh conditions, led to frequent complaints and occasional flight from villages.
- **Emergence of Large Landholders**: Some loyal families or officials accumulated vast estates, forging a new rural elite that overshadowed older feudal-like structures.

19.11.2. Growth of a Modern Bureaucracy

Muhammad Ali's successors, especially Isma'il, expanded government offices:

- **Civil Servants**: Young Egyptians, often from middle-class or minor notable families, studied in new schools or abroad, returning to staff ministries.
- **Adoption of Western Norms**: Over time, government departments adopted European-style procedures—record-keeping, audits, and hierarchical management.
- **Cultural Exchange**: This Western-influenced bureaucracy introduced ideas about constitutionalism, secular law, and social reforms, setting the stage for nascent nationalism later on.

19.11.3. Cities and Cosmopolitan Elites

Alexandria and Cairo thrived as international hubs:

- **European Communities**: Merchants from Greece, Italy, France, and elsewhere established businesses, especially around the Suez Canal's

opening. They formed cosmopolitan enclaves, often gaining extraterritorial rights under the so-called **Capitulations**.
- **Modern Amenities**: Steamships, telegraphs, gas lighting, and paved roads transformed urban life. Cultural salons and clubs, sometimes mixing Egyptian intellectuals and Europeans, signaled a changing urban identity.
- **Social Stratification**: Alongside modernization rose glaring inequalities—ruling elites grew wealthy, while many laborers and peasants toiled under heavy burdens.

19.12. Final Assessment of the Muhammad Ali Era

Though he began as an Ottoman appointee, **Muhammad Ali** created a new dynasty that ruled Egypt well into the 20th century. His reforms laid foundations for a modern state:

1. **Centralized Government**: Power consolidated in Cairo, with professional bureaucrats and a national army.
2. **Economic Shifts**: Cotton exports, industrial attempts, and infrastructure works connected Egypt more closely to global markets.
3. **Education and Social Change**: New schools, foreign missions, and a budding intellectual elite sowed seeds for further transformation.

His successors, faced with rising European economic influence and internal fiscal strains, steered Egypt through expansions and crises, culminating in the country's deeper entanglement with foreign powers by the late 1800s. While the impetus for modernization was real, it often brought severe hardships for peasant communities and increasing debt. The stage was set for continuing foreign intervention, culminating in partial British control.

CHAPTER 20

CONCLUSION

20.1. Overview of Egypt's Long History

We have traveled across roughly **5,000 years** of Egyptian history, from the earliest prehistoric communities on the Nile to the dawn of the modernizing projects under Muhammad Ali and his successors in the 19th century. Throughout this monumental timeline, Egypt experienced dramatic transformations yet retained a core identity anchored in the Nile's life-giving floods, a shared cultural memory, and the resilience of its people.

In this **final chapter**, we synthesize the major eras covered:

1. **Prehistoric and Predynastic Egypt**: Originating with small agricultural settlements along the Nile that gradually evolved into complex societies, leading to the first dynastic unification.
2. **Pharaonic Periods**: The Old, Middle, and New Kingdoms and intermediate phases, during which Egypt built iconic pyramids and temples, developed a powerful centralized state, and influenced neighboring regions.
3. **Late and Greco-Roman Periods**: Foreign rule by Persians, followed by Alexander the Great's conquest and the Ptolemaic dynasty, merging Hellenistic and Egyptian traditions, then Roman governance fostering new forms of administration and religious change.
4. **Christian and Coptic Egypt**: The spread of Christianity, the rise of monasticism, and the eventual dominance of the Coptic Church, culminating in religious schisms and challenges under Byzantine authority.
5. **Arab Conquest**: Transition to Islamic rule in the 7th century, forging new political and cultural identities within the broader caliphate framework.
6. **Fatimid, Ayyubid, and Mamluk Periods**: The establishment of Cairo as a grand Islamic metropolis, marked by monumental architecture, military prowess, and vibrant cultural life.

7. **Ottoman Province**: Integrating Egypt into a vast empire while allowing local elites, especially Mamluk beys, to retain influence, leading eventually to 19th-century reforms under Muhammad Ali.

20.2. Enduring Themes in Egyptian History

20.2.1. The Nile's Centrality

Across all eras, the **Nile River** shaped agriculture, settlement patterns, and religious notions. The cyclical flooding and fertile silt remained a consistent source of wealth, enabling both the pharaonic building projects and later Islamic expansions. Control of irrigation systems often determined political power, from ancient pharaohs to modern governors.

20.2.2. Layers of Cultural and Religious Synthesis

Egypt saw multiple layers of external influence—Libyans, Nubians, Persians, Greeks, Romans, Arabs, Turks—yet continuously integrated newcomers into local traditions:

- **Art and Architecture**: Pharaonic methods merged with Hellenistic aesthetics under the Ptolemies, then with Islamic styles under later dynasties, resulting in eclectic forms.
- **Religion**: Native deities coexisted with Greek cults, transitioning to Christianity, then Islam. Each transformation left behind monuments and communities reflecting syncretic beliefs.

20.2.3. Shifting Centers of Power

From Memphis, Thebes, and Alexandria in ancient times to Fustat and Cairo in the Islamic era, capital cities anchored political authority, each leaving distinct cultural legacies:

- **Pharaonic Capitals**: Heliopolis, Memphis, Thebes symbolized divine kingship and temple-building traditions.
- **Alexandria**: A beacon of Hellenistic learning, trade, and the famed library.
- **Cairo**: Initially a Fatimid royal city, evolving into the seat of Mamluk sultans and later Ottoman governors, now recognized worldwide for its monumental Islamic architecture.

20.3. Political Continuities and Breakdowns

Egypt's story is one of both impressive continuity and sharp breaks:

- **Dynastic Successions**: Ancient pharaohs established a pattern of monarchic rule. This tradition of strong centralized power reappeared under Mamluk sultans and later Muhammad Ali's line, albeit in different forms.
- **Intermediate Phases and Conquests**: Repeatedly, internal strife and foreign invasions shattered centralized power, leading to "intermediate periods" or transitions—whether from Old Kingdom to First Intermediate Period or from Fatimids to Ayyubids.

Over the centuries, Egypt's population learned to endure new rulers, adopting practical ways to maintain farming, local commerce, and cultural identity amid changing regimes.

20.4. Socioeconomic Dynamics

20.4.1. Land and Peasants

Throughout Egyptian history:

1. **Rural Focus**: The majority of Egyptians have always lived as farmers, reliant on the Nile floods.
2. **Taxation and Labor**: Whether building pyramids for pharaohs or paying tribute to Ottoman governors, peasants provided the backbone of the economy.
3. **Migration and Hardship**: Droughts, locusts, plague, or excessive taxation periodically forced farmers off their land, fueling internal migrations or labor revolts.

20.4.2. Commerce and Trade

From antiquity, Egypt capitalized on its geographical position between Africa, the Mediterranean, and the East:

- **Pharaonic Expeditions**: Sailed to Punt or Lebanon for incense and cedar.
- **Hellenistic and Roman Eras**: Alexandria thrived as a maritime hub linking the Mediterranean to the Red Sea.

- **Islamic Period**: Cairo replaced Alexandria as the primary metropolis, fostering trade with sub-Saharan Africa, the Indian Ocean, and Europe.
- **19th-Century Integration**: Cotton exports under Muhammad Ali's successors tied Egypt to European markets, intensifying foreign influence in local affairs.

20.5. Religious Evolutions and Tolerance

20.5.1. Polytheism and Temples

For most of pharaonic history, a complex pantheon of gods shaped temple-centered worship. Large estates attached to temples influenced politics and land use. Notions of divine kingship underscored pharaonic authority.

20.5.2. Christianity and the Coptic Church

- **Spread of the Gospel**: By the 4th century, Egypt was largely Christian, with distinct monastic traditions (e.g., St. Anthony's desert hermitage).
- **Coptic Identity**: After the Council of Chalcedon (451 CE), Egyptian Christians mostly followed Miaphysite theology, becoming "Coptic." This identity persisted under Islamic rule.

20.5.3. Islamic Dominance and Pluralism

Post-7th century, the majority gradually adopted **Sunni Islam**, though Copts and other minority faiths continued. Periods of tolerance alternated with occasional bouts of discrimination, but a broad cohabitation of faiths characterized Egyptian society, especially in major cities.

20.6. Intellectual and Cultural Contributions

Egypt's contributions to world culture are immense:

- **Architecture**: From pyramids and Karnak Temple to the mosques of Ibn Tulun, al-Azhar, and the grand Mamluk complexes, Egypt's built environment is a testament to evolving aesthetics and engineering feats.
- **Literature and Scholarship**: Papyrus texts from pharaonic times, Hellenistic scholarship at the Great Library of Alexandria, Christian writings in Coptic, and medieval Islamic works at Al-Azhar create a continuous chain of intellectual output.

- **Art and Decoration**: Tomb paintings, Greco-Roman mosaics, Coptic iconography, and Islamic calligraphy reflect a seamless fusion of forms spanning millennia.

20.7. Resilience and Adaptation

If there is a single overarching theme in Egypt's history, it is resilience. Despite foreign conquests, natural disasters, plague outbreaks, or economic crises, Egyptians repeatedly adapted to new conditions. The continuity of language, cultural memory, and reliance on the Nile held society together, even when regimes changed.

20.8. The Significance of the 19th-Century Transition

Muhammad Ali's reforms signaled an important pivot point:

- **Shift Toward Modernization**: Introduction of standing armies, mass education, industrial attempts, and new economic policies.
- **Deeper Global Integration**: Cotton exports, the Suez Canal project, and foreign loans bound Egypt to European markets and influences.
- **Loss of Autonomy**: Mounting debts led to direct interventions, culminating in the partial foreign control that overshadowed the late 19th century.

This laid the groundwork for 20th-century developments, including nationalism, struggles for independence, and further transformations—though these modern evolutions lie beyond our scope here.

20.9. Looking Forward

While this book focused on ancient through early modern history, one might reflect on how each era's legacy persists:

- **Touristic Heritage**: Monuments from pharaonic tombs to medieval mosques draw global visitors, sustaining cultural pride and identity.
- **Pluralistic Society**: Coptic Christians and Muslim communities still coexist, each preserving centuries-old traditions, joined by other minorities.

- **Cairo's Enduring Role**: The city remains a vibrant capital, shaped by layers of Fatimid, Mamluk, Ottoman, and 19th-century architecture, each telling part of the national story.

Closing Reflections

Egypt's history is vast, complex, and inspiring. From the earliest inhabitants who harnessed the Nile's floods to cultivate crops and gather in proto-villages, through the heights of pharaonic civilization, the Greco-Roman and Coptic eras, and the sweeping changes of Islamic dynasties and 19th-century reforms, the story remains one of constant adaptation and cultural fusion. Over millennia, Egypt has proven its ability to synthesize diverse influences—absorbing and integrating them—while forging a distinct identity that resonates across time.

Though we have not ventured into the 20th century and modern era, the foundations laid in the chapters above illuminate how deeply the past shapes Egypt's national character. The **resilience of Egypt's people**, the pivotal location bridging continents, and the abiding significance of the Nile have all ensured that, regardless of who claims power, Egyptian society endures and evolves with each new chapter of history.

In concluding this book, we honor the millions of unnamed Egyptians—farmers, artisans, scribes, mothers, soldiers, merchants—who lived through triumphs and trials, from prehistoric hunts along the Nile to the 19th-century transformations. Their collective efforts form the tapestry of one of the world's oldest continuous civilizations, leaving us a legacy of wonder, beauty, faith, and perseverance that continues to captivate imaginations everywhere.

Printed in Great Britain
by Amazon